WHAT PEOPLE ARE SAYING ABOUT "FINDING HIS VOICE"

"I only meant to read three chapters but I couldn't put this book down. I was captivated from the first chapter and read the entire thing in one sitting! This book was truly written for such a time as this. Jen takes the reader on a powerful journey about life, love, and loss in a way that will bring you to tears, have you laughing out loud, and jumping for joy at the goodness of the Father."

– JAX CARDENAS

"I read it straight through. The entire thing, in a couple hours. Your story shares a remedy this world needs. What an amazing testimony of overcoming. A testimony that communicates the secret to experiencing freedom in life from the bondages we find ourselves in, in this world! This is a book worth reading and rereading!"

– KARA GROVE

"There are soooo many self-help books out there on how to "find your voice again" after tragedy strikes. So many authors and motivational speakers talk about how they gained THEIR strength by finding THEIR voice again. They are totally missing it and don't realize how much they are limiting their very healing, progression, & growth. We eventually become stuck and can only go so far on our own. Jen shares this deep and emotional

journey of losing her dad to suicide with us and recognized the very truth that she can't keep fighting through life on her own. She discovered God in the most unlikely places and REALLY encountered Him through every twist and turn of her own journey. He walked with her every step of the way, and with every decision she CHOSE to listen to HIS voice no matter how hard it was or how painful the situation was, and that made all the difference! In fact, it ended up setting her free from the heavy chains of the past and lead her to breakthroughs and a life of success! Through every chapter we see HIS voice move and speak over her and leading her closer to finding her purpose! This book will inspire you to stop asking the creator of the universe so many WHY questions such as, "why did this happen THIS way?", "What did I do to deserve this?", and "Why did this happen to ME?!". Listening to our own voice only leads us to being held captive by our thoughts, but more importantly, learn to listen and be receptive to HIS voice that told Jen so many times, "even if I never told you why, could you still trust me?". Jen stepped out in faith and put her trust in HIS voice every step of the way. It was at that place that she found true freedom and a peace that surpasses all understanding by allowing the joy of HIS voice to be her ultimate strength. She is such an inspiration and after reading this book, I am encouraged to examine my own life by taking a step back to quiet my own voice and learn to hear HIS voice speak through every season of my life. Do you feel stuck and still burdened by the pain of your past? Do you need some motivation on how to overcome and start to live a more fulfilling and purpose driven life? Do you want to learn to discover HIS voice while learning at the same time how to impact the lives of those around you in a positive way by sharing your story in a way that leads others to healing and breakthrough as well? Then THIS is the book for you!"

– SARAH LOFLIN

"Re-reading when Jen shared her story on stage at our coach's conference, that was my first event since my mom had died. Hearing Jen's story shattered the wall I had put up. Her sharing made me say, "Okay, let's do it!". And now my life is so much more hopeful than it was. I've been freed from so many things in this last year or so because her story spoke to me in a way others' couldn't. This book, this story is going to help so many more people! Jen is so open and honest! I honestly couldn't say enough good things. I felt so encouraged as I read through her story more! There have been so many times since my mom's unexpected death that I felt totally abandoned and this book helped me see all the little ways His voice has been speaking to me and bringing me hope for my future."

– KRYSTINA JONES

"I had forgotten how dark those times had been for Jen. I walked through life with her as she was carrying *so much heartache and pain. When I see her today and see who she has become, I am absolutely astonished and blown away by who God has molded her to be. Also it has built up my confidence in the Lord that He is good and always faithful! By reading this book it can literally save a life. Those that are in deep despair and pain can find hope and healing with Jen's story. God has done amazing things in Jen and through her that you have to believe He will do the same for you!"*

– LAURA HILP

"I can't even get through the acknowledgment section without tearing up. Once I started the intro, the encouragement and hope Jen expressed felt like she was talking directly to me, to my heart. Wow, I can not believe who this woman has become. Actually I can, because I know her!! And she has changed my life too!! I use to feel so hopeless, just going through the motions of life in a fog of numbness thinking it will never get better and honestly what's the point of even being alive? Because of Jen I have reconnected a relationship of hope and joy that I truly thought was gone forever. She has not only inspired me to not give up, but has help guide me to a life worth living! Jen has been such a pivotal power player in my life. She is filled with joy, enthusiasm, and a love for peoples hearts like no one else. If you need encouragement right now, read this book!! This book will speak to your heart. It will wake up the joyful child in you and show you exactly

how to start changing your life for the better. This book speaks to all the years of pushing people away, feeling like no one will understand and the deep ache of loneliness I've felt and maybe your feeling too. This book will give you hope and saying "I am NOT alone and we got this"! Whenever I am feeling down, I can pick up Jens book and immediately feel encouraged for brighter days and strength through Him. If we just take time to listen to the Voice, He will handle the rest. This story is proof that even in the times of despair or confusion, if you just listen and have a little faith you will be rewarded beyond measure. "

– ELISSA SAWAYA

"I couldn't put this book down it was so engaging. A passionate autobiography from tragedy to triumph, Jen eloquently takes us on her personal, painful journey of losing her earthly father then learning to hear her heavenly Father's Voice. You'll be encouraged and uplifted to work through your own losses through that same Voice which led her out of darkness into a new successful, fulfilling and joyful life!"

– KERI THEWLIS

"When I first met and read Jen's book. I loved her honesty and courage to keep walking through the fire of pain and loss, all while determined to overcome whatever came her way and find new ways to learn how to be a better version of the life she was living all while helping,

teaching and encouraging others do the same. While having a huge loss of my own knowing that Jen had walked this road before me and that if she could keep moving forward, have hope, strategies and relate to my pain in many ways and the pain of my children or anyone going through any kind of loss and grief that there was hope for better days ahead for us and that is what Jen's sweet words of encouragement and life example did for me, it gave me hope and helped fill in the cracks in my heart. Jen's life has been a beautiful testimony of how brokenness can become beautifully broken."

– JENNY WILLIAMS

"This book is raw and real. It reveals the love of the Voice so profoundly. It was as if it was speaking directly to me as I turned the pages. I could hear the Voice echoing all that I needed to hear at this time in my life. This book is powerful and speaks directly to the heart."

– KELLY KENNEDY

"The story contained within this book is one that will have you crying, laughing and cheering for Jen's triumphant journey through immeasurable pain. Her ability to draw you into the story will have you captivated from start to finish and leave you wanting more."

– SARA FISCHER-REYNOLDS

"I read Finding His Voice while sitting for hours in a

chair getting chemo treatments for stage four metastatic breast cancer. I totally forgot where I was and what I was there for. The lessons I learned in this short captivating book are valuable and usable. The inspiration I received is priceless. I was inspired to truly see, listen to, and care about those around me; to not long to skip the hard times and miss out on what God wants to show and teach me; to live each minute of my life more intentionally; to keep my faith and hope in our good God who has proven Himself faithful; to always have a heart for others, especially the poor, the hungry, the hurting; to make sure the people I come into contact with know they are loved and valued by God and by me; to run towards my fears; and, most importantly, to seek His Voice in each moment and to find it in each and every one. Jen is a courageous warrior woman and beloved daughter of the King. Not only does she run towards her fears but she vulnerably shares her battles with us so that we, as well as everyone around her benefits from both her defeats and her victories. She has truly found "her" voice: it is the voice of God."

– KAY VANDYKE

"These days it's hard to find a story that you haven't heard before. BUT THIS, my friend, is a story that is so incredibly unique. It captivated me from the start and I kept wondering...what crazy/amazing....cramazing thing is going to happen next?!? At the same time it constantly kept me giggling out loud and ALSO inspired me to NEVER let go of the dreams that the Lord has put into my heart! This story is a testimony to the deep love that God has for his children and the beauty that occurs when you start to rely on His Voice! And if you ever want to give up...this book will show you that IT'S SO WORTH IT to work through the hard things in order to get to a place of peace and belonging. Jen's beautifully, wonderful story teaches us what can happen when we start listening to the Voice and moving in the direction that will lead us into the MOST amazing and adventurous life we could ever want!"

– BECKY GRITTON

"Not only did Jen take me on a journey through her own personal struggles and growth, she pierced my heart directly. I can relate to her feelings and emotions in other areas of my life that I was not willing to face. She showed me how to have courage to acknowledge those realities and face them! Just think of how much better the world would be if we all invested that much into bettering ourselves and dealing with the weights that have held us back! Jen is an inspiration and I am so proud of her for finding her inner warrior!"

– JENNIFER YATES

"This book is a book of inner healing. Jen inspired me to literally take the leap of faith where I've been lacking zeal. The countless actions she took, regardless of the immense pain & fears she experienced completely moved my spirit. Her suffering was not in vain. "His" power surge outlet radiates through her to copious others. This "Voice" of rescue she shares is a lifeline to me where other "imposter voices" have no doubt consumed the minds of millions. I encourage anyone who is going though "devastating" personal and/or emotional struggles to read this book...a real "prescription for facing tragedy. Her decision to help others to succeed, while shifting focus inspired me to take the necessary action to also experience freedom. This book will no doubt have lasting influence, bring fulfillment, and destroy the yoke of bondage."

– REBECCA HENDERSON RODRIGUEZ

"I read this book in two sittings. It would have been one but my husband said I had to do other things...like eat, sleep, and go to the office. I dove into this book at a time when I found myself sliding back into depression, a time when I needed the encouraging reminder of the power and greatness of His Voice. For those feeling overwhelmed, lost, unloved? This book is for you. I felt like I was walking these roads with Jen - crying with her in her sorrows, cheering her on in her victories, and leaning in to listen to the Voice that made all the difference in the world."

– KIMMI SPARKMAN

"*Jen is a woman of amazing strength, courage and a true warrior! I am so BLESSED to have crossed paths with her a few times. The whole time I read this book I was weeping. I was reminded of the Yahweh's realness. I was inspired by what he did in her life and how he spoke to me through her story. It's an example of hope, freedom, and Yahweh's promise to us: For I know the plans I'm planning for you. Plans of peace and not of evil, to give you a FUTURE and an EXPECTANCY. Finishing her book made me realize I need to stop being afraid and share my story too. It's hard work and I'm so grateful Jen persisted! Seriously! I connected with so much of what Jen wrote about and the parts where she wrote what the voice said to her, it was exactly what I needed to hear too.*"

– JENNIFER KIMURA

"*Jen draws you in through her vulnerability and keeps you there through her story telling and humor. This book will have you laughing and crying, but in the end you will be inspired. It's a must read for anyone who has a loved one they've lost through suicide or has struggled with thoughts of suicide. This is a story of hope, and ultimately courage to move towards the One who can change your life. I felt encouraged and inspired throughout the book to be real, vulnerable and transparent in sharing my story with others. I feel hopeful after reading Jen's story that my life and voice matter.*"

– APRIL BROWN

"Jen's story of overcoming devastating losses, and rising to levels of success that she never thought possible is truly inspiring! The changes in her, and the fruit in her life are definitely a true testament to the power of God and the power of trusting Him and having faith in Him!"

– DANA WINAND

"As Jen takes us on her exuberant journey, looking back at her life and heart with hard-won honesty, there are many moments of both laughter and sorrow, even deep pits of brokenness, but through it all I was impressed most by the impact of a life fully yielded to God -- that Voice that is constantly speaking life into our ears, even when we plug them up with our fingers. If we choose to listen, the impact first begins within us, but like a smooth stone tossed into a pond, the ripples radiate ever outwards in concentric circles, affecting our family, friends, and even perfect strangers. This book is an extension of Jen's ripple which her heavenly Father can turn into a great and awesome wave! I hope you will take the plunge and be blessed."

– TINA WOODEN

"It was funny, eye opening, encouraging, inspiring and liberating! This book demonstrated just how much opportunity lies in cultivating new relationships. We can learn so much when we open ourselves up to see the world through someone else's eyes. I was reminded to be bold *enough to share my own story and that in our differences lie the opportunity to offer something uniquely inspiring. I was struck to repentance and liberated of a shame I hadn't realized I was still carrying. This testimony served as a reminder to heed the loving warnings of our heavenly Father, and as an eye opener to the past warnings I had ignored. Because in this book, I was able to forgive myself and release the guilt I had been holding on to. I envisioned my past self through His eye's. I saw His sorrow from my hurt, His disappointment for my foolishness and his delight in my accomplishments. It encouraged me to be intentional in really SEEING others and to stop being so afraid that they might just see me too. I was inspired to act out my faith, regardless of how other people may perceive it. Last but not least, the words in this book confirmed that He is still at work amidst our present day struggles and He will not abandon us despite our shortcomings. Thank you for your boldness to write and share this book! You are the example of an overcomer and I have no doubt you will continue to inspire countless people around the world with your funny personality, big faith and heart to help others!"*

– TIFFANY OSBURN

"Finding His Voice is a hard book to put down. I started and ended each day with it. I couldn't wait to get home and read more. I was sad and sorry for all Jen went through but our God is awesome and she is incredible! I

couldn't be more proud of her. Jen's writing is inspiring. Her book brought light to her voice, His voice and the victory she found in knowing the difference. It was honest and heartfelt. Her joy radiates off the pages when she truly discovers God truth's and it is moving to see how Jen has chosen to let His voice move her to be an inspiration in the lives of others."

– CRISTA HORLING

"Finding His Voice is going to be an essential tool in helping the fourteen to thirty something deal with the suicide of a loved one or friend. I was led along an unexpected emotional adventure, complete with inner voice conversations which were followed by new action, spiritual awakening and heart healing. All this in a gentle, nudging, you can survive it too narrative. It's priceless. Honestly, I think this story should someday be a movie!"

– SUZANNE HANDLEY

"Jen made me laugh and cry with her life story. What a beautiful tribute to both her Heavenly Father and earthly one whom have formed the person she is today! I'm so grateful for her openness and honesty about some pretty tough situations in her life. I will highly recommend this book to those I know."

– DAWN RICHTER

"Just finished Jen's book and I have emotions I wasn't

expecting. I made one of the most important decisions of my life a few weeks ago and had been questioning what it would take to stay the course. The way Jen wove specific 'downloads' from the Voice in each chapter culminated in that Voice speaking directly to me to confirm I'm on the right path, doing exactly what I'm called to do, and not to waver. This book will impact your life…maybe like running into a brick wall, or, like me, by subtly infiltrating my heart to deal with a root issue I didn't know was still there (you'll hear about those in chapter 23). Jen's fun loving yet transparent and soulful writing style will keep you engaged and you'll learn something new about yourself!"

– SHANE ROBY

"This story of a journey through grief yet laced with comedic interjections had me in tears and laughing out loud within the same 15 seconds. Authentically raw and vulnerable, Jen's story of making meaning out of tragedy and allowing it to propel her toward Greatness will inspire any one open to the message to claim the freedom that exists for each one of us."

– BETSY SAWAYA-CHAVENEL

"I normally read before bed and fall asleep in 5-10 min. When I got this, I finished reading the ENTIRE book that same night. It's amazing. I couldn't stop! Knowing Jen before and through this experience I was always (and continue to be) amazed at her COMPLETE trust in God. Life was not made easy for Jen, she met obstacle after obstacle and yet her faith never wavered. Her consistency through it all has brought her true joy and a better life. This is an honest look into the heart of a true world changer. Sincerity with a humorous perspective, it's a captivating must read!"

– LAURA PIGORSH

"I read Jen's book with tremendous expectation, and was not disappointed! In telling her story Jen helps us understand the Voice of God as it speaks to and through a creative mind. What would that voice sound like, what would it say? In looking back on events in her life, both good and bad, Jen clearly learns to understand those events through the eyes of God, growing her faith amidst blessings. (Three-quarters through this book I had to send Jen a digital hug!) And in learning to both hear and listen to the Voice Jen finds tremendous joy in the rest of the story she and God are writing! While some of Jen's experiences may rub the more conservative reader the wrong way, she shares them honestly and with no regrets, knowing they are part of her story, a part of who she is today. Seekers, stop seeking and take some time to read Jen's story. You might just find what you are looking for."

– JIM DYKSTRA

"I once heard someone say, "you cheer loudest for

the success of those who you've been through the struggle with." I have personally had the privilege of standing in the gap with Jen. Watching how God showed up so hugely in her life is a story I will never forget. Jen has always been one of the strongest believers I know, staying faithful though many of life's hardest struggles. But wow, there is even more to her story that I didn't know! Her book draws you in and you won't want to put it down. If you're looking for an inspiring page turning story, this is it. I guarantee you won't regret it."

– BRITTANY NOLL

"Your book really felt like it came from your heart, and you really put yourself out there to help others. It really touched me how much you have worked through, and it makes me feel like I can work through the hard things in my life without fear and listening to His voice instead of my own. You rocked my wold and inspired me to keep working on my dreams."

– EUNICE BOERBOOM

"I just finished reading Jens book and it makes me want to jump up and Praise God with all my might! I have seen her grow from that shy little girl into a bold woman of God! I am so proud of how she has let His Voice lead and been so willing to surrender and follow! This book is absolutely an answer to prayers. I prayed for her when she was small, knowing that God had given her talent.

I prayed for her when tragedy struck, as so many others did, knowing that God promised to work all things for her good. I prayed for her over her adult years. This book-and all the work He has done over 16 years- is all an answer to those prayers. Thank you so much Jen, for showing yourself so fully, for digging so deeply into your heart, and for constantly listening for His Voice. Like Jen, I wish I could speak to my younger self such messages of love and hope. Reading this book is a balm and a torch-it soothes and heals but then lights a new path. Listen for the Voice that Jen is listening to. He won't stay silent."

– REBA HAMILTON

"Reading this book was surreal. There were many parts where I felt like I was reading my own story. The message is clear. God's voice is encouraging and the people we meet on our journey is not an accident. This is a story of a bold and courageous woman who took action and has incredible results."

– KIMBERLY GASTON

"A truly inspiring book for anyone, but will certainly reach the heart of someone who has suffered great loss. We are not alone, He is there if we are truly listening. Jen has learned to sow the Word, and she has reaped what she has sown, humbly. How blessed are we to read her story, be inspired, and know that we have the same opportunities. Listen, Read and Pray. Those sowing in tears, shall reap *with songs of joy. Tehillim (Psalms) 126:5"*

– DEB SILOR

*"I loved the book, your heart, your vulnerability, &
your faith & love for God. Thank you for showing me
what it means to put all of your trust in Him, listening to
His voice. You are an inspiration to so many! Love you!"*

– CINDY DEBOER

*"Wow, wow, wow!! Great insight, great message, great
author."*

– OJU AJAGBE

*"I cried as this book put words to the emotions that
I myself never found, and I burst into laughter equally
as much. I don't know if I've ever read about someone
having such faith in God."*

– HANNAH GROTES

FINDING M~~Y~~ HIS VOICE.

AN OVERCOMER'S JOURNEY
FROM SUICIDE TO SUCCESS

JEN HORLING

Finding His Voice
An Overcomer's Journey From Suicide To Success

ISBN: 978-1-7349204-0-6
Printed in the United States of America

Cover Design by: Sponge Designs, Inc
Photography by: Jason Little Photography

www.sponge-designs.com/the-overcomers

**An overcomer's journey.
The secret was not about finding me,
but finding Him.**

DEDICATION

To the Lover of my soul. The one who said, *"we got this, you and Me."* Not only did we do it, but it has been far more than I could have ever imagined it would be. This book is dedicated to You. May You use it for far more than I could ever imagine, and do the same for another.

ACKNOWLEDGMENTS

Dad, thank you for who you were. Thank you for showing me what an authentic and passionate love for the Father looks like. You loved Him more than anything else in this life. I saw it in how you pursued Him, how you dove deep into the scriptures, searching out further context, culture and history. I'll never forget your hunger for Him, and the joy that radiated from your entire being the day you called home while touring the holy land a few years before your passing. You were home then, and you are home now. Thank you for your radical love! Not only for me, but for the world. You showed me that we're far more capable of extending our hearts and our hands to our fellow man than we even think we are. Thank you for the gift you gave me of what it looks like to SEE others, to SEE beyond ourselves and how you lived that with every single action that you took. You were and are a true hero, to so many. Thank you for your service, as a Vet, a Fireman, an EMT responder, and a Father. You were sacrificial, humble, and passionate. A warrior for the hearts and well-being of others. Your legacy lives on. An entire book could be written about JUST the way you loved.

Mom, thank you for not giving up. Your battle has been quiet, but your fight so loud. We made it. We not only made it, can you believe what life is now?! Thank you for pointing me to the truth the entire journey. That our God would be with us. You were right. You were so right. Thank you for the quiet tears, and the painful prayers, I know He heard every one. Thank you for the hugs, the walks, and the talks. Thank you for your selfless love, my entire life. For your listening ear, and your compassionate heart. I never doubted that I was loved deeply by you. Thank you for loving dad! In the many years that have passed, I can see more and more why and how he became 'home' to you. Thank you for choosing to trust that our God is redeeming still and believing with me for all that He will yet do.

Grandpa & Grandma, you loved relentlessly. I can't imagine how proud you'd both be not only by getting this story out there but of everything that's happened since your passing. Thank you for your sheer delight and intentional interest in every single art project I giddily shared with you throughout college that I was working on. I wish I could show you all the things I've worked on since. Thank you for believing in me, not only throughout those years but ever since I was little. You made me feel like I could do anything. Thank you for how much you loved our family, and our entire extended family. Thank you for the countless Sunday dinners with the whole family, and all the birthday and holiday gatherings. You kept our family close. You kept love close.

To my friends, to name you by name would be far too many your impact. Thank you for your genuine acceptance, love, grace, and friendship. Thank you for the countless hugs, prayers, and my favorite…laughter. You make life fun. Thank you for putting up with all my weird off the wall ideas WE MUST DO, words that come out strange, and desire to put you into a costume or paint you blue. Thank you for being there. In every season. Thank you for walking with me in the hardest ones and not giving up on me. Thank you for listening, even when you didn't understand. Thank you for pouring life into me.

Steve & Becky D, Matt & Tracy D, Don & Sarah V, Cindy F, Kay VD, Josh B & Laurie D, thank you. There's no doubt in my mind I wouldn't be who I am today, let alone survived the seasons I was in if it wasn't for your intentional influence. Thank you for your hearts. Thank you for your diligence, your commitment, and your willingness to share your lives and your own relationship with the Father with me. His timing is so perfect, and you were perfectly timed in my life. In my families life. And now, look what He has done and continues to do! That is the impact of your influence and your sacrifice.

Dani J, wow! Where do I even begin? Coach, you were the game changer. I'll never forget the day I sat in the front row of my first conference staring into the face of the most stunning and powerful heart I'd ever met. You showed me that everything in my entire journey that I had been hoping for, every stirring in my spirit that ached for the more that I know this life is and my God was, wasn't just a hope or a prayer. You showed me it was truth, and it was tangible. You were living proof of it all. But you didn't just prove it to me, you cared enough to show me how. And not just me, but countless of hundreds of thousands around the world. Your heart is unmatched. You are diligent, committed, passionate, sincere, genuine, and full of Justice! He continues to use your story to tell of who HE is. You are a vision of His strength, confidence, faithfulness and his epic love. This is who you are. He delivers, He redeems and it is powerful through you. I can't imagine everything you have had to continue to fight through to continue being as transparent as you are all these years. But I was finally transparent with my whole journey because of you. I was set free. And in that freedom I know this story is going to help inspire hope to so many more fighting to find their voice. Fighting to find His. Your courage gave me courage to do what I thought was the impossible. May freedom and His voice continue to ripple far more than you imagine because of who you are.

Chad K, thank you for your honor through the entire journey of not only helping get this book out there, but since the day I walked into the DJC community. You have continued to speak life into me. This story wouldn't be what it is without the depth to which you partnered with the heart behind every word, and your patience with all the weird bunny trails they took you on. You saw every sentence and breathed further life, clarity, and power into them. Your ability to see life, speak life, and make a story shine even brighter is such an incredible gift. I couldn't have done this without you. Like a jeweler, you saw what I knew this story could be and refined it. You were the earthly Father it needed, yet another beautiful story of Him, his heart and protection amidst the journey.

Diane M, Tammy P, Mary W, Linda P, Shawn H, Chris S, Shane R, Mark H, Hadassah A, Charles & Tracy Z, the entire DJC, thank you for your acceptance! Thank you for your hugs, smiles, words of LIFE, and how you believe in me! Thank you for being a safe place. Thank you for how you inspire me! You are the most amazing human beings on the planet. You work harder on yourself than anyone else, and you're willing to do what it takes to fight for your future, your families, your community and the world. You show the world that life can be better, is better, and all the while not portraying to the world that you're "perfect". You're real, and I love being in a community where it's celebrated the more freedom that comes as we shake off the mud in our lives. Every time I'm amidst you, I feel like I get a glimpse of what Heaven will someday be. You guys are true Overcomers. You are the hearts that will change the world. I believe in you! Let's do this.

TABLE OF CONTENTS

FOREWORD

BY DANI JOHNSON

Are you at a place in life wondering "Is this all there is?" Do you have something in your past that is so horrific that you might not even know how to talk about it? Are you drenched in pain and heartache, feeling trapped and don't see a way out? Have you ever been tormented with sleepless, restless nights?

If your answer is yes to any of these questions, I'm so excited that you are holding this book. Why, you might ask? Well, deep down inside, you know there has to be more—and maybe you don't know what it looks like, or how to get it. This book is going to show you what it looks like, and how to get it. You are going to get free from the seemingly unending questions, like:

"Why did this happen?"

"Was there something else I could have done?"

"What if I get hurt again?"

These questions have kept you stuck, but they also hold a way to get unstuck!

I am so proud of Jen. As I've watched her, I can see that, more than anything else, she wants to help people. This is a woman who is taking a risk by putting her vulnerabilities out there for the world to see, simply for the purpose of helping others be free, as she has been made free.

Jen has experienced real pain, confusion, shame, and fear in her life. She knows the sleepless nights of a tormented mind. She has had to overcome the pain of suicide, grief, and severe trauma. Rather than staying trapped in her own heart and mind, she learned what it takes to experience the life of freedom that she desperately wanted. She learned how to get over her "stuff," and how to take responsibility for the things she had the power to change, instead of chasing after things she could not. She stepped up, rose up, and has done great things with her life. Jen's story will show you how to navigate the pain of your past, so YOU can have a life of freedom, too.

As you read this book, Jen is going to inspire you to push past what's holding you back. You are going to learn how to flip your mindsets, flip your words, and flip your life. You are going to learn how to flip your deepest fears into amazing experiences of joy!

If Jen can go from being paralyzed by the fear that controlled her, to living in good health, light, love, acceptance, freedom, mercy, and grace, YOU CAN TOO! Let this book challenge you, and read it to its last page, so that you, too, can begin your own journey of freedom.

Friend, I believe in YOU -- and I'm excited for the deposit that is about to drop into you. Jen's story is not over, just like your story is not over. Let Jen's story encourage you to become all you were designed to be. You are worth it. Your family is worth it. Your community is worth it. Your world is worth it, and we NEED YOU. So, lets get reading...

INTRODUCTION

There are stories to tell.

People matter.

If I could go back 15 years to the day I stared tragedy in the face and tell myself not only what's ahead in this life, but what it is NOW...wow! I wouldn't believe me. I would be in complete shock, and honestly, would probably say, *"how is that even possible?"* or *"That does NOT sound like me."*

But that's precisely it. I would tell her:

"Anything is possible! Dream as big as you can. Don't let anyone tell you otherwise. The pain you are in right now will pale in comparison to the joy you will radiate through your entire being and your very life!

I'd tell her that the same Voice that softly spoke to her in her darkest moments will never leave her and will continue to speak and lead her life to amazing things!

I'd tell her not to give up because the other side is worth it!

I'd say, 'That Voice you are hearing in the back of your soul is going to blow you away by just how much He shows up in your life and answers the cries that are in your heart—even the ones you don't know are there yet! He knows you more than even you know you and He loves you! He loves you more than you can possibly imagine.

"Don't give up! There is a future you are meant for, that you are designed for! And just when you think 'how could it get any better than this?' He'll show up again and say 'Oh, you think that's cool, Jen? Watch Me now!'

"I've seen it.

"I've seen it countless of times.

"I've heard the things He's going to say to you. I've watched Him wrap Himself all over your life, and walk with you every step of the way. I've watched Him pull you through seasons where you

thought you couldn't go on. I've seen Him carry you. I've seen Him fight for you! Even in seasons where everyone else thinks, 'We can't believe what He has done in your life in the afterglow of tragedy.' MANY years later, when you're still fighting for the MORE you know this life is and your God is.

"I've seen Him answer your prayers and lead you to RIVERS of His flow! Rivers of His love! Rivers that will lead you to the dreams your soul cries out for every single night as you fall asleep, and every day as you dream for more. Every hard-working day, as you put your whole heart into everything you do!

"The God you believe in is out there—the One who met you and spoke to you that night, the One who sees everything you've been through, and continue to go through...

"HE KNOWS.

"He sees every tear. He hears every cry. He understands.

"He is close to the brokenhearted. He is with you.

"Don't you doubt it for one day—not even for one second.

"I bless you with hope! I bless you with peace. I

bless your heart and your future with healing!

   "He is at work!! You press on! This is not the end. This is just the beginning!"

Friend, this book is for YOU.

Why?

Because you are called to be FREE. I know what this Voice has done in my life in the 15 years since my life was turned upside-down, and I want Him to do the same for you.

If I can overcome, YOU can overcome.

CHAPTER 1

"Step Up, Rise Up, And Do Something Great With Your Life!"

The preface

I remember people saying, *"does she even talk?"* It probably didn't help that I hid behind my mother's legs as a kid, and even had to repeat pre-school because I clung to the teacher every day.

PRE-SCHOOL (just wanted to make sure you read that right).

I feared people. In High School, I was the girl who never wore makeup or had any particular style. I let my hair grow to my butt until college. And I definitely didn't talk to boys (they had cooties).

Public speaking? Forget it! I'd rather die. In fact, a friend once tracked how nervous I was by tallying how many times I said *"um"* in a 5-minute speech (seventy-five).

I started college completely broken by tragedy. And left college still trapped with lingering thoughts of suicide. Why? I feared loss. I endured verbal and emotional abuse, having death spoken over me.

Like most college grads, I entered adult life totally broke. But even as my career took off, everything about it felt like such a lie! Oh sure, I looked successful, but success isn't about what you make. But even if it was, I was still broke! I had many limiting beliefs and didn't even know it!

I even viewed myself as a person of BIG FAITH, seeing God do the miraculous in my life, but in reality, I was letting labels (both from others and from my own mind and heart) have rulership over my destiny and didn't even realize it.

So how did this God-loving church girl with BIG FAITH, whose life was SO MESSED UP, become:

- A BOLD lover of people?

- A woman of unshakable faith, who uses her voice to help others?

- A woman who fights for others?

- A woman whose heart has been set free, and no longer feels trapped?

- A woman who runs toward fear?

- A woman who is thrilled when asked to speak, and rises to each occasion?

- A woman who is full of LIFE?

- A woman whose outer appearance shouts of confidence, creativity, boldness, and joy?

- A woman who is covered in tattoos?

- A woman who has paid off a crazy amount of debt in a super short time?

- A woman who is now the CEO of a company that "gets to be creative, while we help the poor?"

- A woman who is leading that team to freedom?

- A woman whose business tripled, and then doubled again? (Man, by the time this book reaches your hands, it will probably have quadrupled, septupled, or superstatsticbombastic-doodled! I think that's a Disney song. Supercalifragilistixpsuperstasticbombasticdoodled. Yea that's it. Have I mentioned how great I am at remembering song lyrics? Well that should tell you.)

- A woman whose friends and families lives are being transformed?

- A woman who believes, that anything is possible?

How did this happen? It's easy. Well, the answer is easy. But it's what you do with that answer that makes all the difference.

The answer was not in finding myself, but in finding Him—in finding (and continuing to find) the voice of my Savior in every step of the journey.

He spoke to me in every season, and that's what this book is about: His voice, not mine. The voice of the Father. But boy, did I have a lot of work to do in every instance and season that I found it.

And sometimes, to be totally honest, I fought it!

Whaaaaaat?!?!

Oh yeah, there were seasons I listened more to my own mind and heart than to Him. And yes, there are plenty of moments where my often aloof and highly-imaginative brain caused me to get lost in daydreaming (at the most inopportune moments) about this Voice and all it was doing.

Once, I was in a drive-thru and when they asked for

my order, I accidentally started praying into the intercom, *"Dear Father...WAIT! I mean I'd like a burger, small fry, and a Diet Coke, please. Sorry, I was lost in thought about someone else."*

And we're definitely not going to talk about the time I drove right past the pick-up window after paying for my meal, never even getting my food. Let's just say my mind was often elsewhere.

Then, a bomb went off in my life. That's when things really got exciting. I know that sounds backwards, but it's true. So much of this life we live passive, un-engaged. We just show up, and sometimes we don't even do that! Isn't life supposed to be more than just being present?! I think the human race is in real danger because 98% of the population is just "showing up." God is speaking to them about bigger things, and they don't even notice!

Crazy, right?

It doesn't have to be that way. You and I get to choose what we're going to do with this life. You get to choose what you're going to do with this book after you read it. It can encourage you, or it can collect dust. My hope is that it gives hope to someone going through their own season of pain. I want you to be able to see the other side and tune in to that Voice, so He can guide you through it!

I also hope that you go one step further and find me.

"'Find me?' That seems pretty forward, Jen."

You're right, it does. I mean, find me at the place where the "bomb" went off; and find me again at the place I believe that Voice brought me to 15 years after tragedy hit. Find me in the place where all the dreams and desires that were on my heart found their catalyst—a coach who viewed her God in the same way I did...BIG!!

This coach, who served as the catalyst for my dreams, was living proof there are no limits on what you can do to help people—to the tune of hundreds of thousands of lives being changed and impacted. I'm not just talking about the ones who attended her conferences, but the countless poor around the world—rescuing children whose lives had been ripped away from them in the sex trade, and providing homes, food, and water to the poorest of the poor around the world.

Finding this coach was a game changer. It was the "bomb" I desperately needed. Have you ever felt desperate? I was desperate to figure out how I could help people more. It kept me up at night. Every night.

I was at the place where I felt that, if I couldn't spend my life doing that, then what's the point of being here? I was getting opportunity after opportunity to speak LIFE into hurting people within the creative/entertainment industry, but I was beyond frustrated! I knew there was more…something…I just didn't know how to find it. I devoted myself to training. I found someone who truly cared about people and was doing it. She put me on a course that continues to exceed what I ever thought truly possible. This coach was Dani Johnson, and I'll talk about her often in the following pages, because she was such an important part of my transition. I know I'll continue learning from her, attending conferences and working on myself, because one thing she said was, *"Work harder on yourself than you do anyone else, and you'll be unusually successful."* I want to be unusually successful so I can serve the hurting.

People are dying. Those people matter.

People are feeling broken and defeated. Those people matter.

You matter.

CHAPTER 2

"I Delight In You"
The Story Intro

"Whoa whoa, okay! Wait a minute, Jen! How'd you go from here to there?"

I promise I'll take you through the whole journey. First, let me tell you about that subtle Voice I was hearing and what He said at one of Dani's recent conferences.

(WooHooo, time travel!!! Yep, time to put the party pants on. It's the only way to travel. Mine have lots of pockets. Anyone want some tots?)

She challenged us to think about what needed to change in each of us. Everyone has things they can work on. I totally broke down. In the front row.

Bent over, with tears dripping from my eyes and snot dripping from my nose, forming a puddle on my iPad on the floor. Exactly what everyone wants to happen in front of hundreds of people, right?! But I realized the best thing I could do with that opportunity was to EMBRACE it! Not care what anyone else thought, and just give 100% of myself to that moment. It brought about a major win.

Friend, we're given choices every day. What you choose to do from minute to minute determines whether you're going to win or lose. Be ALL-IN.

Part of this exercise was to walk through the steps of forgiveness. I started by forgiving myself, but then I turned my attention to forgiving my dad…more (you'll learn more about that soon). When I got to the part when I had to say, *"I forgive you, dad, for not being here NOW,"* the words coming out of my mouth surprised me. I completely lost it. I didn't even realize I needed to say that until that moment.

Have you ever had things come out of you that surprised you? I one time exclaimed to a friend I had only met minutes before, *"you smell like meat."* Not exactly an ice-breaking statement, but then again, we were hiding in the cabinets underneath a giant metal buffet table, as part of a game. That comment, while it surprised us both and made us chuckle, made sense at the time. I'm talking about the surprise statements that expose the roots hidden so deep in your soul that you don't know they are down there.

Later that night, Dani invited us to come to the front of the room for a time of prayer. I went up and put my face to the floor. Having grown up in church, I was familiar with times of prayer like this. But something powerful happened in that moment. Dani said, *"Ask Him what He wants to say to you."* As strange as this might sound, I had a vision. The Voice that had been with me in every season of my life quietly painted a visual in my mind. It was like a cinematic movie playing in front of my eyes.

In this movie, I could see a pair of feet walking through crowd of people around me, but I couldn't see anything above the knees. I could only see the feet slowly stepping between the people. I could sense that this person was observing the brokenness throughout the room. Then I realized, it WAS Him! The Voice! He stopped in front of me, stooped down and picked me up like a father would pick up his little girl. In this vision, He threw me into the air like a joyful daddy, spinning me through the air in circles, and taking pure delight in me.

I looked in His eyes and asked, *"what do you think of*

me?"

He answered: ***"I love you more than the moon and the stars. And I designed you to shine brighter in the darkness than they do. That's how much I love you. That's how BIG the purpose is that I have for you. That's how I designed every cell of who you are. Every season, every part of your story, is for that purpose. And I will work with you to accomplish it. You are my moon."***

+++++

Let me take you back 16 years. Blooooooogelelspeowbbbpoof! (Come on now, I can't be the only one who makes sound effects in their head. Don't push the red button!!! I pushed it.)

It's my senior year in High School, and it's the Powderpuff (girls) football game. My heart is beating out of my chest. The referee's whistle shrieks and the center thrusts the football into my arms. I scan the field to see who's open. I see my window—there's a break in the defense. I make a run for the end zone. I can see it getting closer. Almost there. The next 15 seconds tick by in slow motion. I charge forward with all my might and run across the goal line. Touchdown!

Before I can make a victory dance, I'm whisked up from behind (not like a kitchen whisk. That'd be weird.

Arms and legs caught everywhere in between it all). More like a tornado: you don't see it coming and BOOM! It's there and you can't stop it. I feel myself being lifted right up and thrown into the air from behind, like the cow in the movie, *Twister*. Thankfully, no houses or neighbor dogs blew by. Someone had been so overjoyed they ran right onto the field, chased me all the way to the end zone, picked me up and ran around with me in their arms, jumping and screaming. It was a total whirlwind. I look back to see who has me in their arms, and it's my dad.

+++++

I grew up with a great affinity for sports, and played everything I could. I grew up watching basketball with my mom and brother and felt awed watching Michael Jordan in his glory days. I wanted to "be like Mike," and often forgot that I was in high school. I played basketball with some pretty great people. I learned a lot about myself.

Now, I know you have this image of me with mad skills, shooting on one foot, and dunking with my tongue out, but I pretty much sat on the bench. I did stick my tongue out anytime I played; that's true. And weird. But the bench was my end zone.

I loved my team, I loved the sport, and I cheered my heart out. I knew that, if I were out on that floor, I'd want my teammates yelling my name, so that's what I did: I yelled my name.

No. I seriously cheered for my teammates.

After games, people who had been sitting in the stands would often say, *"Jen, we could hear you from the bleachers!"* Maybe I should have yelled their names, too (I don't like to leave people out). At the end of the season, as they handed out awards like "Most Valuable Player" or "Best Defense," I was given the "Barnabus Award." No, I wasn't given a man. (That would have been nice, but I was much too young for that. I wasn't even talking to them at that age. They were scary.) Moments later, they reassured me it was an award for encouragement. When the coach went on to describe the spiritual meaning behind it, I was beaming. I cared about people. A lot. But it wasn't until years later that I realized just how much they mattered.

Why am I telling you all this?

+++++

It was my first week of my first year of college and I was living at home. As I pulled into the driveway after my morning class, I could tell something was different. The driveway was crowded with unfamiliar cars. Mom greeted me at the front door, and as the tears streamed down her cheeks, I began to cry, even though I didn't know why yet.

It was the strangest occurrence. I could feel the connection to her pain, and knew something was really wrong. I clutched her to me, without taking notice of the family and friends who filled our home.

Out of the cleft of her broken heart, the words slammed into my chest: *"It's just going to be you, me, and your brother now."*

My lungs burned. My heart pounded. Everything went silent and dark but my mother's words. Those massive words felt like the slam of a gavel reverberating through me. Suddenly, I gasped for air and the scene around me came back into focus. I heard myself wailing, exclaiming, *"What happened?!?!"* Not only had my father abruptly passed away, he had chosen to end his own life.

He had shot himself in the head.

CHAPTER 3

"I'm Not Going Anywhere"

Death's Events

My dad.

The man who ran onto the field and threw me into the air in delight! My hero. The decorated military veteran who had served in Vietnam. The passionate fireman and trained EMT responder. The devoted dad. The man who loved his family, his God, his church family...even strangers! The man who could do anything and often did. The man with the biggest heart I'd ever known. The man who had traveled to other countries to help people in need. The man who would jump at the chance to help anyone in an emergency, and packed his bags and gear to help when the World Trade Center fell in New York City. The man who, on Christmas Day one year, wrapped up our family car with a giant bow and gave it to a missionary family in our church who needed it…and we didn't even have plans for the next one! He cared more about helping others!

He's gone?!?!?!?!

I remember holding mom. There we stood, each seeking support from the other in the entryway. Neither of us had any strength. Neither of us knew what to do next… or even what to think.

Out of the corner of my eye, I saw people. The house was murmuring with the hushed voices of aunts and uncles, friends, family, and our pastor. I spent the rest of that tragic day in a blur, barely aware of being wrapped up in the arms of family and friends. Tears were just pouring out of me. Friends came and left, followed by strangers. Each hour, another family member became aware of the awkward sense that there was nothing more they could contribute. They faded quietly into the darkness.

Every thought that came to me terrified me: dark images of our lives without him. The thought of my father taking in his last breath squeezed every last tear from my eye. How do you process the idea of someone you love in so much pain? How do you process the image of someone you love with a gun to their head?

Earlier I shared with you the things I wish I could say to the old me—the 15-years-ago me on the day of tragedy. This was THAT day. That's the me I was speaking to: the girl staring this tragedy directly in the face. Man, I wish I could have spoken over her and into her that day. I wish those words had been there that day.

There were voices speaking that day: some spoke life; others, death. But there was one Voice speaking that day that still speaks today. It speaks in a whisper straight into my spirit, through people, through nature, through songs, through dreams. It weaves a message that He was with me then and still is today!

You might be thinking *"I didn't know what to say to her!"* OR *"I don't know what to say to anyone going through pain like that"* It's OK! You're not responsible for knowing what to say in those moments. As you continue to read, you'll hear how the VOICE spoke! It's that Voice that I clung to.

The shock and trauma of that day could be seen on all our faces. We all seemed lost in a sea of puffy, red, and raw complexions. More people came and more tears came. I can still see the faces who came that day. I remember where they were standing and the expressions on their faces as they walked up to the house and in the front door. I can remember every single moment. I probably looked like a drunken, sun-scorched sailor who needed a eye-patch, peering out of the corners of my weary eyes.

The heart-wrenching didn't end when they were all gone. In fact, when the last person said goodnight, the silence that followed was absolute. I had never felt silence or darkness like that before. I hoped the dawn would make the day of sadness end, but it didn't. The pain and uncertainty were fresh in the morning...and all that week.

I was not ready to say goodbye. I was still in complete shock and disillusionment. You don't just "move on." I remember driving out to a Men's Warehouse store with my brother so that he could get a black suit for the funeral. We both expressed how little clothing mattered anymore. Nothing seemed to matter much. The sorrow of losing someone made even the necessities of life seem trivial. Not that we debated going nude (...okay, maybe I did.) I really didn't care what we wore.

On the drive back, the song, *"I Can Only Imagine"* by MercyMe, came on the radio. My brother turned the volume up as loud as he could. I sobbed in the backseat the entire ride home. Years later, that song still made me cry. Maybe because I realized the next time I would see him would be in the eternity they sang about (well, other than the time I "saw him" at the home improvement store...or his doppelganger rather. Boy, did *that* give me a spook!). In my dreams, he has come back and said, *"Just kidding, I was hiding!"* Okay, THOSE dreams have never been that lighthearted. But, oh, how I have wished he was just hiding. I haven't found him yet (despite being spectacular at doing so with Waldo).

If I could go back to that day, I'd say:

"Jen!! You won't know this until years from now, but someday, they are going to make a movie about that song and its origins. You'll learn that day that the songwriter wrote it because he had lost his father! I've seen the tears you will cry that day as you watch that movie. The tears you cry that day will be different. Your heart will be different. Everything about you will be different. And the view of you that I see is more beautiful than YOU can imagine. Your Father, God—that Voice—loves you! You won't believe what He is going to do in your life over the next few years! The tears you will cry that day will be happy tears of reflecting back, because you will SEE even more powerfully how He showed up for you in the dark time. He was there more than you realized.

Imagine, another person was so inspired, going through his OWN loss, that he wrote this song and pushed through his pain to produce and share a message that would help you—a stranger going through the same pain at the same time! That Voice knows you need that message right now. He sees your pain. He's going to walk with you through it— and beyond it!

I bless you with continued healing. I bless you with revelation after revelation of how this Voice is at work in and around your life.

I bless you with the strength to do the same for another someday."

+++++

The first visitation was awful. Life had felt so surreal the previous few days, but the visitation was the first time we had seen my dad since the tragedy. Nothing can prepare you for seeing someone you love lying in their casket (especially when they're dead; but I'm not sure why you'd lay in it alive, unless you're a vampire). I remember walking into that room and having my breath taken away (not my blood, so I guess that means he wasn't a vampire). Usually this only happens when you're hit by a baseball. Having your breath taken away, I mean. Granted, I did get hit in the head by one years later, but at the visitation, there was no one with a mitt in sight.

It wasn't a baseball that hit me. It was the suddenness of my emotions. His death was suddenly real; there was no longer any possibility for life within him. Any chance that it was all just a bad dream was over.

I felt cheated! It wasn't right...he wasn't supposed to be gone yet!!! I just wanted him back.

My knees immediately became weak and my body locked up. I was frozen there, ten feet away from his casket. There was no room for denial with his body lying right in front of me. I desperately wanted to cry out that THIS could NOT be happening! This was my dad!!

How I wish I could go back to that day. I'd say:

"You're right. This is your dad. And this was NOT what the Voice wanted for him. But I can tell you this: he was a great man. You know that. You know he loved his heavenly Father more than anything else in this life!

"There is nothing you could have done. This was not your fault. What that Voice is going to do with what happened will someday eclipse the sight before you now. He sees you. He sees the shock you're in and He is at work!

"I know the message that's coming in a few minutes! Just hang on! THOSE good words will root alongside the bad. The Voice will fight for you! I've seen the day He wins! I've seen the day you win! The day you set yourself free! I see the way you will

walk. I see your heart. Your burden will be so light. I've see the FREEDOM and lightness you will walk in the day the bad root gets uprooted. I've seen the day you will cut that tree down. I've seen the gentle way in which the Voice will speak to you before and after.

"I've seen the father figure the Voice will place beside you that day—the one who reminds you of your dad: a strong man with a good heart and an incredible love for his family. I've seen the joy on your face with tears still wanting to burst from your eyes. Those tears will be different. You will look to the sky and exclaim, 'You are so good!!'

"I bless the new root that's about to take hold in your heart! I bless that root with LIFE. I bless that root with so much power that you become unstoppable. Your faith becomes unstoppable. That Voice becomes unstoppable within you!"

+++++

I wish I could say that I knew the best way to handle that moment, but I didn't. This was the chance to see his face one last time, an opportunity to talk to him, but I knew he was not there to listen on the other end. It was not how I wanted that moment to go, but there I was, stuck.

A root took hold in my heart: from that moment on, I struggled with saying goodbye if something felt final. My body and mind always went into shock.

The visitation went on for three days! There were lines snaking around the outside of the building every day. Part of me wondered if we should be handing out refreshments or a "fast pass" (I would have wanted a snow cone, and maybe five dollars to play Ring-It To Win-It; the giant stuffed animal I won at a carnival needed a friend). My brother and uncles walked around outside at times just to see how long the lines were. They couldn't believe it. Fire trucks came from every single station across the city. There were so many faces and kind words.

One in particular stood out: Laura, a close friend at that time, was in line. Laura was one of the most caring hearts I knew, a friend so typically full of life and laughter. That day, she was more subdued. I saw her of the corner of my eye as she crossed the room toward me. I will never forget the hug she gave me as she whispered in my ear, *"I'll never let go."* Those words echoed in my mind. Through her words I heard the Voice, my Savior. I saw a glimpse of Him. I felt loved, reassured that He was my Rock and always would be. I felt a friend who would bring healing, a listening ear (even if they didn't understand) and amazing encouragement to persevere.

The visitation and funeral were beautiful. Our pastor spoke of dad's life and testimony. Never before had I been so proud of him; never before had I wanted to tell him so badly. I should have walked right up to his casket and told him, but I probably would have taken him home with me, too. Some things you just don't do at funerals.

To this day, I don't remember much else of what was said. I was in a complete fog. So many people came to say their goodbyes at the service that we had lines out the door, through the entryway, and snaking around the building. Firemen from all across the city came in uniform and on the engines to give their sympathies. There was one question that gnawed at me: if he could have seen how many people loved him, would it have kept him from pulling the trigger?

If I could go back to that day, I'd say:

> **"That's a great question, Jen. We can't control anything that anyone else does, only the things we do. And this question you're asking will be one that helps drive you into who you become, what your heart becomes. I've seen the refining process He is taking your heart through. You are in the HOTTEST part of the fire now. You are being scorched, melted down through one of the hardest battles this life will bring. It will burn, but it won't consume you.**

He is with you now and will stay with you through the whole process.

"You will RISE! You will be victorious for the hearts of the hurting! Never ask whether you should do something when opportunity to help arises. Just do it! You know that every second counts! Every life matters! And you will fight!

"You will fight for others' lives, because you will be on the other side, and you will know it's worth it! You know that they are worth it!

"I bless you in those future battles. I bless you with VICTORY! I bless all the hurting hearts with healing!"

+++++

The initial week was so difficult, but I remember thinking at that time that the Voice brought us through our shock. I had wished we didn't have to have the service and visitation so soon; I was still taking it all in. My heart had been shattered into a million pieces, and I didn't really want life to go on in this new way.

The tears hadn't stopped for days, but at the visitation they stopped suddenly, and I believe that was that Voice's doing! He gave us the grace to get through it. A passage that came to my attention those first few days spoke directly into my soul. It said that this Voice was a ***"Father to the fatherless."*** It was exactly what I needed to hear. The absence of my father shrouded me in fear, but this fear was immediately replaced with an unexplainable peace. I knew this Voice was with me and I didn't need to be afraid. The guidance, admiration, and relationship left void by the death of my father was becoming filled by the presence of this Voice. Never before had I had such a desire to know this Voice so closely and share with Him the thoughts that filled my mind. Never before had I cried out to Him from such despair.

As the nights turned into mornings, and days became the weeks and months that followed, I found myself looking to this Voice more and more.

CHAPTER 4

"We've Got This, You And Me"

The College Years, Trauma, and PTSD

The first few months after his passing were awful. I felt sorrow for the first time. Real sorrow; the kind of sorrow that affects you physically. I never really knew what that word meant before. My heart was not just heavy; I could actually feel a physical weight that seemed to constrict my chest. My shoulders felt as if I was being pushed down from above. I remembered scripture about giving your burdens to God, but never before had I thought you could literally feel physical weight from them. Sorrow became my blood clot...my 290th bone...my sixth finger. Whoever killed my father needed to die. Oh...wait. (Sorry, terrible movie reference.)

I felt it in my throat. Whenever music struck an emotional cord, or words of worship hit me a certain way, I would fight so hard to hold back the tears that my throat would literally begin to close. I battled to breathe. I struggled not to bust into tears, to the point of physical pain. I know many of my friends saw tears throughout those first few years, but I wondered how many could really see the weight of them. The fight was so intense, so real, that I was doomed to have a "six-pack" that I desperately didn't want—a six pack on my face.

I'm 21 years old, going through heavy grief. Not just grief, but now dealing with the effects of trauma. I asked my uncle Don, *"What do I do now?"* He gave me the best answer anyone could have, and it catapulted me into the exact direction I needed to go: to be a circus clown.

Okay, maybe that's not what he said. He said, *"Jen, you don't have to do anything…you can do anything you want."* I felt free. Circus, here I come!! Just kidding. Not only did I feel free, I OWNED what I chose to do from that day forward. I had no idea what I wanted to do leaving high school, but I knew that I hated math, science, history. I wanted not only to enjoy my life, but to get more out of it! I knew that if I didn't do it, who would? My protector was gone. It was up to me to move forward.

I went to a small private high school with no art

programs, but I began to realize that I always felt alive any time I did anything creative, so I decided to take some art classes. I loved every single one of them, and saw something igniting inside of me.

Yeaaaaaas, let's light that fire!

I later discovered that there was even a profession where you could be creative and not be poor! Fancy that! Then I got really excited. *"Graphic Design...what's that?!? Oh, yea. I want to do THAT!"*

So, I'm sure you've already guessed what I did next: I canceled all that and joined the local circus. NOT! I pursued, and later graduated with, a design degree. But my college years proved to be some of the toughest. The emotional battles were intense. I'm not going to lie; there were times it might have been nice to have a spare circus lion handy. Then again, I kind of did. Professionals with fancy titles and degrees call it Post-Traumatic Stress Disorder (PTSD). It's real. I've lived it. It halts everything else...unless you have a Voice calling you through it.

Not a day went by, those first years, that I didn't think of him. His image or name seemed to be permanently ingrained in my brain. Maybe someday they'll have an eraser for that.

I would go to a movie with friends and come upon a

scene where someone kills himself, and my body would go into shock. It would panic. I'd immediately start to sweat and my breathing would become heavy. It was like my body was making an immediate connection to the last time it went through those emotions. I walked out of so many movies those first few years, with my emotions seized up, and no expression on my face. My heart and mind couldn't handle it.

Whenever that happened I'd be lost. If we had been in a group, I'd always get a phone call as soon as I got home. Laura would call to ask if I was okay, and listen as I cried. Over time she knew what would strike my heart. She could tell by the cast of my face. I'm sure other people knew, too—I was always the one with wadded tissues and running mascara (and for some reason the only one who got attacked by the creatures in the movie, *Raising Helen*, and left the movie a zombie. If you haven't seen it, there are no zombies. It's a drama. The zombies were in my past. I could've used 10 lions that time).

+++++

The first wedding I attended after his death brought it all back to the surface. The day dad died, I was sitting next to my aunt. Between sobs I gasped, *"...he won't be there to walk me down the aisle!!!"* Girls grow up thinking about their wedding day and planning all sorts of details, but I had NEVER been one to give it a thought...until that day.

I was too busy dreaming about getting drafted into the WNBA, traveling the world, having a FUN creative career, or becoming a grocery store bagger (I know I'm weird, but stuffing grocery bags looked so fun to me).

Suddenly, for the first time in my entire life, I thought about my wedding day—at my dad's funeral. How weird is that?! Many weddings have come and gone in the years since, and every time the dad walks his daughter down the aisle, I am still so heartbroken. If anyone wanted an emotional wedding walk, all they had to do was look at me. I may look young for my age, but many must have wondered if I was the mother of the bride with how hard of a time I was having. That's why, when they asked who gives this woman away, I always uttered under my breath, *"...her father and I."* Okay, maybe I didn't do that, but I am guilty of hiding pain with humor.

If I could go back to that day, I'd say:

"Don't be afraid. I've seen the vision He's going to give you for that day, many years from now; the simplicity of it, the connection between you and the Voice. The love you have for it will far exceed the love you have for your earthly father. When that day comes, you won't want a BIG wedding anyway—you never really have. But the beauty in the simplicity of every moment will take your breath away.

"I can see you standing there, ready to 'walk to the new', and you CLOSE YOUR EYES. As you walk with your you eyes shut, let the Voice of his stillness lead you to the new, just as He's led you your whole life. Follow in complete faith and trust that he has you, even though you can't see it! He has you, just as He always has! He will have you then just as He has you now!

"I've seen the journey your heart will go on, the battles it will go through, the lies it will break free from, the confusion that almost killed it. You will be victorious! He will be victorious! I've seen the beauty of what He uncovers within you, as you take His hand and follow Him to the Holy Land. What He uncovers within you there will fill you with new excitement and LIFE as you anticipate this day.

"Take heart; this is not the end, this is just the beginning! I bless your heart. I bless the journey it will take. I bless the finished work. I bless the complete heart that's on the other side. I bless the NEW! I bless the love that Voice has led you to. I bless it with LIFE, and life abundant! I bless it with joy! I bless it with fun! I bless it with adventure! I bless it with power! I bless it with impact! I bless it with even MORE hearts reached around the world with healing."

+++++

I struggled with images, like the shock of the initial day it occurred. I remember pulling into the driveway full of cars and wondering what was going on: it couldn't be a garage sale—James Bond wasn't there, and the last time we had a garage sale, he helped me with everything (OK, maybe that was just a dream). I was a freshman in college, and I did not understand why there were so many cars in my driveway, and that image has always stuck with me. I had stopped on the way home for a fast food burger for lunch, and I still have no idea what happened to it. The neighbor boy probably ate it (or maybe James Bond ate it when he left).

Since that day, this image of a driveway overflowing with cars has always made my heart instantly start to beat rapidly. Years later, I pulled up to another family member's house, and seeing a driveway full of cars made my heart start to panic. My breathing became short and my mind raced. Nothing was wrong, but my mind instantly made the connection to the shock it associated with that sight. I walked into my cousins' home with tears in my eyes, asking *"what's going on?!!"* Everything was fine, but everyone immediately knew what I feared.

I'd picture my dad's arrival at Heaven's gates (and my own) a lot those first years. With dad, I saw him collapsing to his knees with his hands on his face and tears streaming down his cheeks. Those same tears often plagued my mind with the image of his death that day. I was never a morbid person, but felt so suddenly thrust into such painful and clear pictures of death and the crossover to eternity.

Every time the image of my father in his last moments on Earth came to mind, it was so painful. He was so alone...and I could see him sobbing as he put the gun to his head. With the crossover, I pictured him kneeling before the Father, sobbing, his pain washing away as he finally sees his Savior, the one he loved more than anything.

I pictured it every time I would hear the song, *"Come to Jesus"* by Chris Rice. It was sung at our church the Sunday after he died. The words are so powerful. I pictured dad as I heard the words, *"...and with your final heartbeat kiss the world goodbye, and go in peace and laugh on glory's side, and fly to Jesus, fly to Jesus, and live."* My heart was pounding in my chest that Sunday and tears streamed down my face.

When I pictured my arrival at Heaven, it was much of the same, but my tears cascade at the sight of my earthly father, outstretched arms that race to embrace him.

If I could go back to this day, I'd say:

"He understands. He knows the dreams and sights that are plaguing your mind. But take courage! Do not be afraid. I've seen the NEW visions and dreams He's going to give you! I've seen the countless times he has moved you to tears by new sights—sights of what's to come, sights of his goodness, sights of redemption, sights of JOY!

"The current images and visions will fade in time. Not only will they fade, but He will destroy them. He will wipe them out completely with the NEW!

"And those new visions...wow! You're going to want to see them! Not only see them, but, with great anticipation, see them lived out in your LIFE! They are coming! Press on! Fight! Fight every day to continue stepping toward the new!

"The love you have for your heavenly Father is going to become even greater than your love for the earthly one.

"I've seen your face the day you get to meet that Voice in Israel, the day your soul meets where your RESCUER's spirit resides the most! It will be indescribable. It will be worth it!

"I bless your mind. I bless it with protection. I bless it with discernment. I bless it with wisdom. I

77

bless it with knowledge and understanding. I bless it with visions and images that it give it life and not death!"

+++++

Despite the images, I no longer feared death like I did as a child. I knew Heaven awaited me, but death terrified me when I was little. Of course, growing up, I may have had a fear of socks with seams on the ends, buttons, and our youth pastor (he was a tall man, I thought he was going to eat me), but death was different. Death was the unknown.

After dad died, that ratio completely flipped. I longed for eternity. My fear was replaced with an intense longing to be with the ones I had loved and lost. I looked at life in a new way, telling friends that I wanted to go first.

I should probably get it off my chest that I said that to one particularly competitive friend more than others. The way we competed, I wouldn't have gone down without a fight. At one point, she claimed, *"I could kick your butt at anything we did. I could eat more sand than you. I could catch more minnows with my teeth than you, and even walk across the highway blindfolded and get hit by fewer cars than you. I would dominate in all these normal games."*

78

The point was, I wanted to leave this Earth before they did, before anyone else that I deeply loved died. I wasn't ready to die, but I for sure didn't want to go last.

If I could go back to this day, I'd shout:

"NO!!! The pain you are in will end. The intensity you feel will end. There is so much LIFE ahead of you. If you could only see what I have seen: the joy you'll find; the freedom from pain; the excitement for what's ahead!

"Life and death is in the power of the tongue; don't speak death over your future! You don't know what it holds! I cancel those words with the authority of the Voice! I cancel every utterance of them and I bind them. By the name of Yeshua I send them to the pit!

"I bless you with LIFE! I bless you with long life and life to the full. I bless you with companionship. I bless you with friendship. I bless you with community. I bless you with so many amazing hearts surrounding you that you won't want to leave them! And the day you do, I bless you with the gift of getting to speak blessing over them."

+++++

That wasn't the only degree of my morbidity. While

I don't even know if that's a word, I found myself doing things not normally done by someone so young. Someone who should be looking ahead at their life instead of already looking back…from the end.

I started writing, because I knew, someday, it would help someone like me.

A lot of the depth and description of emotion that you are reading in the retelling of what happened is because I journaled what I was feeling as I went through it. It's crazy to think that here I am, where it's being put to purpose. That's the thing; the Voice that spoke to me that night was redeeming it all…and he continues to.

As time passed, the effects of the tragedy started showing up in my life. So many people commented on how strong we seemed, and that they were amazed at how we were doing. But I suspected it wasn't anything that we had done; it was simply a result of having no choice but to keep living. The "amazing endurance" people saw in us was really just the daily choice not to give up. It was nourished by the friends around us…and that Voice.

I also believe that having been so actively involved in my church during high school positioned me where I needed to be for when trauma hit. I went to everything; activities, events, service nights, mission trips. My life was, *"Hey, Jen, can you paint the youth walls"* nights, and,

"Hey, Jen, can you untangle and then re-tangle all these lights and then just stand there holding them above your head" nights. You name it, I'm game. The leaders became family to me—sources of safety, wisdom, and community I would need. To this day, I thank the Voice for those times. They helped to steady me in the years that followed.

What we went through rooted in me a new desire to succeed. Every day, I had to make the decision to go one step further. I was given daily opportunities to show that this tragedy would not define us. I had a choice.

Running and working out became the zone where I processed the battles in my mind and heart. At times it felt impossible to release the pain. My desire to have dad back outweighed everything else. When I found myself in moments of intense desperation, I let the pain take its course. Fortunately, those intense moments were not continuous: daily battles became weekly battles, shorter and further apart, until finally, only OTHER events triggered such moments of intensity. It was a process, but I saw (and experienced) the destruction true sorrow can do to a person's mind and body. It attempts to destroy it.

I knew I did not want to be defeated by grief. I made the CHOICE to find joy, passion, and excitement in life, and I knew I didn't have to do it alone. I knew that Voice was with me.

If I could go back to this day, I'd say:

"Yes!!! This is your zone. I've seen the things this Voice continues to speak to you as you physically push yourself to the limits! I've seen the breakthroughs that happen. I've seen the release that happens! I've seen the inspiration that comes. He will continue to speak to you through those moments. Embrace them!

"He sees what's on your heart and knows that you are intentionally taking care of your physical state because of the passion inside you that's igniting you more and more saying 'this has to be meant for more!' There is more He has planned for you and you are preparing yourself to be ready, to be healthy.

"As you continue to prepare your physical body, He will prepare your mind! His timing is so perfect!

"I bless your body with physical fitness! I bless your body with health! I bless your body with longevity! I bless your body with the strength and stamina of a warrior meant for battle! You will be fit for it, your entire life!"

The most important fruit of this season of trauma is how my faith found its anchor. Those who know me best may remember me saying, *"God's got me,"* in response to many things through those years. God became my ROCK. It was His voice calling to me over the roar of that painful day, and whispering strength to me in the moments I felt alone without my dad: ***"Jen, we've got this...you and me".***

CHAPTER 5

"Take Every Thought Captive"

The Crossroads

It would be easy to conclude that my college experience was not a normal one. I wasn't a partier, I didn't sleep around (that's a whole other story we'll get to later), I wasn't obsessed with SpongeBob Squarepants, and I had no interest in doing what everyone else was doing. I was pursuing something. I had zero interest in using my design degree to help sell stuff. I had been through trauma. I wanted to help people who were hurting.

Countless times, I saw that Voice drop opportunity after opportunity to serve the hurting with my gifts, and in those moments, the flicker of what would become a

BLAZE started brewing.

It started with simple things:

Sending a bouquet of flowers and a heartfelt card to a woman I barely knew who suddenly lost her dad to a heart attack.

Speaking to a suicidal woman on the request of a desperate mother who wanted her daughter to hear what suicide does to those left behind. I couldn't control the tears that day, but I know that woman is still alive today.

One time I sent a giant get well card to a friend who had major surgery, but I asked random strangers to sign it, instead of people she knew (I didn't even know many of them). One was the woman who took my order at McDonalds; another was a man buying a hot dog at the gas station. Then there was a man riding by on a Segway in the park...

It wasn't all darkness. My senior year, I won a design competition and was flown on an all-expense-paid trip to New York City for a celebratory dinner with a national magazine. They published my ad in their magazine and our school showed me all around the city for three days, with fabulous accommodations in Times Square.

This might sound crazy, but the entire three days

convinced me that big city lights and flash was exactly what I DIDN'T want for the rest of my life. I needed my life to have meaning and purpose; it had to be about people. This was too important. Life is short and people matter. I believe that Voice spoke to me that weekend, through visuals: ***"What do you want, Jen?"*** The Voice was leading my heart to be specific in what it was looking for.

The Voice was preparing my mind. I can see that in every season. Have you ever wished you could fast-forward to the BEST season to skip the hard times? I know I have, and the temptation is real, but if we do, we miss out on the training. The lessons. The things life and the Voice want to show you. I believe there's a purpose for all of it, for every single season you're in! A purpose for every day you're in! A purpose for every minute!

How's that for a mind twister?

We get so caught up in trying to discern the purpose of our lives when, in reality, I think purpose is found in what we do with every second. What are you doing with the time that you have right now, in front of you?

I even believe there was a purpose for that day I decided to crash a pay-per view party of a famous boxing match with some friends at the last minute. Two friends and I walked into a home in a cul-de-sac that had cars parked out front, thinking it was the right party, only to realize after walking all the way through the house's main level, into the kitchen in the back (passing countless strangers) that we were in the WRONG house. Not only were we in the wrong house, we were in a complete stranger's house. Thankfully, the homeowners were gracious and we all had a good laugh. They even offered us a beer as they showed us the way out. What was the purpose in that moment? TO LAUGH! I'm pretty sure I had never laughed harder with a house full of complete strangers before that moment.

He spoke powerfully through mentors, Sarah and Cindy, who had formed a group for college women. This group helped me identify the Voice in the best way possible: flannographs!!!!!

OK, not flannographs. I was just slightly obsessed with them as a kid.

One of these women poured herself into studying the scriptures in the context of the culture and what was happening at that time. She would say things like, *"Can you imagine being a fisherman at that time?! They didn't have the gear we have today! And helloooooo, there was no electricity! And here you are, fishing all day, and then he wants you to go back out in the DARK and fish on the other side of the boat?! You'd think He was crazy!!! But*

*then, when you did it, and then pulled in BOATLOADS
of fish…wait, where would your level of trust be, at that
point, in who this man was?"*

I loved her because she was intentional. She made sure
we learned the Voice's heart for us. Because of her efforts,
the love I had for that Voice grew exponentially, even as I
battled through PTSD. If it weren't for her, and how that
Voice worked through her, there's no doubt in my mind
I wouldn't be who I am today. To this day, despite being
on opposite sides of the country, we stay in touch, taking
great delight in what this Voice continues to do.

Speaking of preparation, this one still blows my mind.
Remember I said that I was that girl who in high school
would rather die than give a public speech? I had to face
that fear not long after trauma hit. It was lurking quietly
in the middle of the list of required and elective courses for
my major: Public Speaking 201 – MANDATORY.

What?! Mandatory?! I'm sorry, but no. I want to be
a designer; why the HECK do I have to take this? In high
school, I dropped out of history class just so I wouldn't
have to give a 2-minute presentation every week. I took
critical thinking instead. I take my no-public-speaking
skipper-outerness seriously!

I found myself at a crossroads.

I think I know now why the chicken crossed the road. He said *"Yep, Imma skip that! Bye, Felicia!"* What was I going to do? Was I going to be a chicken and let my own crippling, irrational fear stop me, or press through? I wasn't ready for it to be the end of the road, so I had to ask myself the unavoidable question: ***"How bad do you want it, Jen?"***

I knew the answer.

I signed up, and it was one of the best decisions I ever made. Why? Because not only did I pass the class, it cured my fear! It completely flipped the fear. I still recall back to that speech class every time I'm given an opportunity to speak, which seems to be happening more and more. I needed the preparation awaiting me in that class!

That professor didn't just teach us how to give a speech; he taught us how to train our minds and control our thoughts. In other words, to "take every thought captive." If a thought says *"I'm going to suck at this,"* or, *"it's going to be awful,"* FLIP it to, *"It's going to be AMAZING! I'm going to make everyone laugh and have fun!"*

He taught us to speak out loud, to give our dreams life, and to be intentional with our words. He taught us how to go into battle! That every time we were going to give a speech, the result was within our control. He told us to see ourselves presenting and envision how the whole thing would go every time before we spoke!

So that's what I did

I ended up LOVING giving speeches, and I have ever since. How powerful is that? Think about how powerful your mind is, friend! All that power is within you! The difference is what you DO with it.

Again if I could go back to this day, I'd say:

"YES, JEN! This is so huge for you! I know you see it in part now, but wait until you see what I see and what that Voice wants to do with you. I've seen the things He is saying to you now play out, and I've seen the stages it puts you on.

"I've seen the day you step on a stage and SPEAK what this Voice has done to you and through you. I've seen you shout, 'He makes all things NEW!' I've seen the hearts you will impact with that message!

"That Voice is not only working in you, it wants to work through you! I'm so proud of you! I bless your life with more victories just like this one. May they be won with a vengeance. I bless your heart to become even more filled with Him! I bless your voice to SHOUT like that lion the things he wants to say!

I bless your life with hearts that are so ready, they sit with even more anticipation and expectation for what It will do as they receive what it wants to say!"

I would love to tell that younger me about a conversation I had with a complete stranger in Hawaii. Because I believe the Voice spoke through her also. She said, *"The moment I saw your face across the room, I was so struck by what I saw. I asked the Voice, 'what do you want to tell her?' and that Voice showed me you with a bright aura over you. He wants you to know it's His promises covering you, surrounding you. He wants you to know He has you covered. I also saw woman of valor on you. He knows what you have walked through. He's brining you to a new season of victory. Like a lioness arising, your voice is needed. He's been waiting; it's time to step forward. I see you freeing women who are held captive by lies. The spirit of the Voice is upon you, strong. The time is here. I bless you with the victory He sees in you."*

I have been asked countless times to speak. Had I not faced my fears and learned that valuable skill-set in the way that professor was going to teach it, I'm sure I would have declined anytime anyone asked, and all those opportunities to help people would have been lost forever.

But I didn't! I said yes, every time! I learned that I had

to be intentional with my thoughts and feed them life!

I was invited to speak at the Thanksgiving service at our church, so I shared how that Voice had been working in my life since the trauma. Another time, I was asked to speak on a Sunday morning about the impact of what we were learning in the women's group! I was asked to speak in our church's youth group after I finished college and moved into a stage of transition. I had just lost a job, so I shared my story about dad, and how I knew this Voice loved me even though I had lost my job. I knew He had me. A few days later, I landed a better job.

When our pastor left the church, he had been there for 12 years—half my lifetime! How was I one of three people asked to speak? His family and mine had become very close. Their daughter was the one who whispered those words of life to me at dad's visitation.

My college graduation was a day of celebration and accomplishment. But with it came longing to share that day with dad. So many big days were like that: the day my nephew was born, and then my niece. I wanted to share stories of being asked to speak and the words I shared. I wanted to tell him about the day I landed a dream job as an intern right out of college. That empty longing has carried through most of my life's major events. Something was always missing. In a way, I'm grateful that it hurts so much.

It means our love was real. But it also proves that his death was not how life was designed to be.

If I could go back to this day, I'd say:

"You're right! This is not how your creator intended your dad's life to go. His desire was for your family to be whole! He sees you. He sees every tear that you've cried. He has promised to never leave you or forsake you. I've seen the hollow celebrations and I've seen the weight of your heart as you wish to share those days with him. He knows! He knows what you have walked through.

"I've seen the warmth He gives your heart. I've seen the people He uses in your dad's absence. I've seen Him orchestrate moments that will blow your mind with how He addresses that very need. Take heart! He will be with you!

"I bless you in each and every event with His presence! I bless you with a peace inside your soul. I bless you with tears—the good kind—as you delight at what all this Voice has done. I bless you with encouragement. I bless you with the hearts of others, that speak life into the cracks in your heart on those days!"

CHAPTER 6

"He SO Has You"

Early Career, A Passion For People

I landed a dream internship right out of college with an amazing company. The timing was perfect; I wasn't cutting it as a Barista at a coffee shop you have probably heard of. While they loved me and I loved that job, the 4:00 A.M. shifts definitely took a heavy toll. 4:00 A.M is when you forget the cup and fill a sleeve. Whoops! I wish I could use that excuse for all the odd things I did during those years (ok, let's be real, my whole lifetime), but I can't. Some things just can't be explained.

My professors had told us to list out who we would want to work for, if we were given our choice, and then told us to look for them. Who knows what could happen, but it wouldn't happen at all if you didn't try!

So I tried, and boom…MAGIC! No, not magic. I'm not a wizard. I took action, found an opportunity and I went after it. Guess who was with me as I did? The Voice!

This first professional job was with a company I believed truly cared about people, and I could tell that Voice was in it. I met some amazing people—I even had the opportunity to meet the band *"Jars of Clay"* one day at work (because of the kind of company it was, we often had artists in the building). I got to thank them personally for a song they had written that meant a lot to me in the years after dad died. I still remember that day and how I felt driving home. I sobbed, not because I was sad but because I couldn't believe how good the Voice had been to me. I didn't just have a song that spoke to me; I got to thank that band in person for their words. It proved to me that this life wasn't accidental.

But there was a more powerful day with that company. Are you ready for this? It was the day I was laid off from the company! What?!?!?! How could terrible news be one of my BEST memories? The Voice reminded me that He and I had built something important while I was there.

The news came from a woman I looked up to; someone whose heart, eyes, and smile instantly filled my spirit with delight! As I sat there receiving the news, I saw her heart.

I saw a woman forced to "let go" of countless people through the years, and the heartaches and bruises she must have been through. I saw the broken relationships and the pain. I saw a woman of high value, a daughter of the king, with a heart for people. How many times had she been misunderstood?

I knew in that moment I wanted my reaction to the news to be nothing other than GRATITUDE! Gratitude for the opportunity, gratitude to have worked for her and that team, and gratitude for this season the Voice had given me as it was changing. I know she was shocked by my reaction. We sat and just looked at each other with tears in our eyes. We saw Him—that Voice—in each other. As we parted, the next words she said to me were so full of passion and empowerment, I'll never forget them. She said, **"He SO has you!"** What a gift to leave with.

What's crazy to me as I write this, is that I was staring into the face of loss again, but my reaction...well...it wasn't me. It had to have been that Voice, stilling me, reminding me that He had been with me and would continue to be with me in whatever came next.

That very night the Voice had even more to say. That same woman contacted me again, sharing that her heart was in a paradox, one side squeezed and the other filled with great expectation and hope for what was in store for me. She reminded me of Isaiah 22:22 as she shared this encouragement with me:

> "...*what He opens no one can shut, and what He shuts no one can open. I am convinced that you have a critical assignment from Him and I am captivated by it. You are so blessed and so safe. He goes before you. When I looked into your eyes when you were let go I felt like I was seeing my forgiving, gentle, merciful, kind, good, peaceful, hopeful loving Papa. How do you do that?"*

There was more to these words but I want you to hear that Voice within them. I returned the message with more gratitude, spoke LIFE into her, and when she opened the response that next morning it left her in tears (good tears) in her cubicle. We have stayed in touch ever since, celebrating as we have watched that Voice work in each other's lives.

How beautiful is that? How often is anger or defensiveness our immediate reaction to "bad news?" I got to see for the first time what happens when you simply choose to SEE someone—to look past the circumstances and see the human the heart sitting across the table from you. It's absolutely beautiful what happens when you do.

Not only did this "ending" bring about a beautiful

lesson, it actually brought about more work! Would you believe that, months later, I was hired back by this same company, not as a full-time employee, but as a contractor? This happened multiple times. I was given the gift of getting to go back and bless the relationships more. There was more healing there.

Months later, I saw this friend start her own fashion line, I asked that Voice, *"What can I do to encourage this heart further?"* He answered with creativity! I not only wrote a note of encouragement to speak life into this new chapter of her life, I did so by sewing right into the very industry. Wait what?! I didn't just write a handwritten note to her. I sewed what LOOKED like a piece of paper with the blue lines all the way across and going down it out of a piece of white fabric but then on that SEWED paper look-alike I then stitched the words onto the fabric letter. Stitching the words ***"I sewed a little prayer for you today. P.S. sorry it took me so long. I had to learn how to sew."*** I wish I could say that was all my idea, but it wasn't. That Voice, had led me.

Isn't it so much more powerful when we let HIM speak? When we let HIS voice be not only the one we're looking for but the one we listen to, the one we let come out of us. I was learning how to do that.

The times I used my own words have been...

interesting. One time I signed a card, "I am Batowan."

Batowan?! My thoughts exactly—what the heck is that?! I meant to write Batwoman, and spelled it wrong. Very wrong. Needless to say, I find my results are better when I let Him lead.

Many new friendships developed in this new season, and I heard the Voice through each one (although it was most obvious with that one). When I returned to gather my things, another co-worker came up and said, *"When I look at you, I see a woman after God's own heart. I look at you and see what I hope my daughters will one day be! You're proof that someone so young can be that woman."* Talk about a rainfall of emotion. I'm BROKEN, and this is what she sees?! She has to be seeing more than just me. This was what I had to say goodbye to! I can't even begin to tell you how I was able to do that other than to say, again, it couldn't have just been me. That Voice was with me.

I had great hope at that time because that Voice had proven so many times that He was GOOD and faithful. I didn't always have the right answer, but I knew that Voice had them.

It was at this moment that I was invited to speak to the youth group at our church. I shared my story, and how I knew that Voice had me and was able to do more in my life than I could imagine. I remember driving during that time, looking to the sky, and shouting, *"I am yours!"* I had nothing...but I knew I was His.

Days later, a new opportunity emerged, and just as I had shared with the youth group...it was more than I could possibly imagine.

In talking with different connections, I was pointed to a non-profit design firm in another state that was doing branding work for service-related ministries around the world. It was the first of it's kind—how amazing is that?! Well, if you've been following the tug of my heart, you can see at least why I was intrigued. I spent the next years working with this company, as it was a freelance-run operation. I was so thrilled to use my talents and experience alongside this amazing team of people, serving organizations that were doing amazing things for people around the world. I got the opportunity to travel all the way to China as a representative of the company, to help train one of our clients on how to use their brand. It felt like so many of the many mission trips I took growing up. I was in Heaven. The people I met and worked with are still close to my heart to this day.

In this same season I had my first real relationship. Come on now, we all know boys no longer have cooties

AFTER college, so I was safe. But that relationship ended and the Voice taught me a lesson as it closed. He was very specific in how He lead me in this area—the area of my heart. Now, years later, I see it all the more clearly. He was trying to take me by the hand. We had reached the point in the relationship where questions were being asked about our future together, and I felt unsettled in my heart. But still He was leading, prompting. One day, I was reading a devotional from "Seeking Daily the Heart of God" by Boyd Bailey, and this passage hit me like a lightning bolt:

> *"The word of God is our warning and our reward, as we travel through life. Like driving down a highway under construction, we may see signs of warning us of a rough ride, closed lanes, or a bridge may be out. We do not ignore these signs because we value our life, time and automobile. So it is as our body, soul and spirit make their way through this life. We are warned by the Word pending danger and simple faith, we listen and become wise. Obedience to God's precepts is fundamental to successful living, and it is a sin to know what to do and not do it".*

Then I read a little further and it said:

> *"God's principles protrude from the foundation of your faith to barricade you from*

the exits of unwise decisions. Therefore do not force down a door that does not freely swing open on the hinges of God's grace. The teachable grow wise, but the cavalier continues on foolishly. It is better to sleep peacefully in the night with our simple life than to awaken preoccupied by unnecessary complexity. He warns us because he loves us. Do not reject the love of God that may be clothed in an outfit of warning. Rewards remind us of the goodness of God, and his grace is his grandest reward. He gives us grace to become a child. He extends grace to be a faithful spouse, an engaged parent, a loyal friend and a loving leader. We receive grace everyday to forgive more and resent less. It may seem like you are losing, but this is for a season. There is victory, even it is a slender reward of a quiet conscience for your obedience." [1]

As I met with this person and we shared our hearts, this person wanted to continue, but there was that Voice in my head that kept saying, ***"No Jen, stay strong...trust me."*** It was then that I started to learn how to trust that Voice IN SPITE of my emotions. I had to trust and listen to that Voice as heart battles were won. And I'm so glad I listened, because I knew my heart was in another place. There was major work yet to be done, and I believe that Voice knew it. Had I not listened, I can't imagine how much greater pain I would have caused.

That Voice led me in some pretty cool things during those years. He had me send flowers to a friend I barely knew who had lost her dad to a heart attack. A few years later, another friend lost her father to cancer. Not hesitating to do what had been done for me, I knew the holidays were going to be hard for her, so I sent flowers and a personal note saying, ***"I understand, and He understands."*** When I saw this woman weeks later, she beamed. With tears streaming down her face, she walked up to me and asked, *"Jen, how do you do this?"* I replied, *"It gets easier, but the first few years are so hard."* It was one of those moments where, despite the pain you've been through, you know that Voice is real. When you want to cry out how much you still miss the one you lost, instead you shout for joy in the beauty of what that Voice has done, and how that Voice continued to help others.

---

1. Boyd Bailey, Seeking Daily The Heart of God (Wisdom Hunters, September 15, 2013)

CHAPTER 7

"I Understand"

Irrational Fears Rear Their Heads

I wish I could say that I handled my personal life as well as my professional life, but no. Loss reared its head in new ways. And I don't just mean in little ways, like the days where I showed up to work, went to the bathroom and looked in the mirror and saw half a pop tart sitting in the billowing collar of my sweater. Oh my. What would you do if you saw that sitting there?! Stand there and eat it, of course! No, I'm referring to much heavier moments. My friend, Laura was getting ready to leave for her own ministry work overseas. Remember how I said I feared loss? I was grieving before she was even gone. I began seeing a psychologist to try to understand what was happening to me.

People who go through trauma experience "anticipatory grief," if they sense they are about to lose another person within their inner circle. I was absolutely terrified of losing this close friend, and she wasn't even dying!

If I could go back to this season, I'd say:

"Jen!! He understands. He knows what you're feeling. And that Voice is a healer! I've seen the miracles He will do in your life. I've seen what He sets you free from! I've seen the lies and the labels and the limitations you have allowed on your own heart!

"Take heart, He will overcome! You will overcome! I've seen the new vision He gives you for this day, and I've seen you RISE up and shout, 'NO!' to the labels and lies.

"You know your healer, and what He's capable of. You know there is nothing that is impossible for Him to do! He is going to get down into every crevice of your heart, every crevice of your soul, every cell within you, and bring healing until there is nothing left to heal. I've seen Him start the process. He

promises to finish what He starts!

"I bless you with healing in every part. I bless you with power! I bless you freedom! I bless you with broken chains and you run toward your future!"

+++++

I wish I could say that this was the only time I saw this fear of loss appear. I wish I could say I beat it to a pulp and then fed it to those spare lions I mentioned having around, but I didn't, because I didn't join the circus (remember?). No, I saw this beast again—in full force this time.

I had developed a close friendship with someone in another state. It wasn't long before we both felt we should have been friends since birth, because we shared an irregular sense of humor. I'll admit it, our friendship was addicting! We became super close and stayed friends for several years, supporting each other, pouring into each other, and making each other—two broken people—feel seen. It was genuine and emotionally intimate. But most importantly, we made each other bust up laughing 24/7.

It was a beautiful thing, but I got too attached. I know it now, but I definitely wasn't willing or able to see it at the time. It brought toxicity, despite the best intentions. It also brought confusion that I definitely wasn't ready to handle. I handled it horribly, and it created problems in the relationship. Eventually, it ended our friendship. Well, I wasn't ready to let go, so there was fighting. It was ugly. After handling the loss of a job so graciously, I totally messed up this loss. I held on for dear life!! I dug in my nails (that I didn't have) as deep as they could go.

Maybe it would have helped if my nails had been longer? Or if they had sparkles? A little bling? Who doesn't like bling? Or maybe baby sharks on the end that would bite her?

Never mind.

The uglier this battle not to loose this friend got, the more it spiraled. It ramped up to verbal abuse, and threats. The death of a friendship. The threat of no more contact. I thought I had done everything the "right" way, only speaking life through the abuse and threats. But the truth is, I wasn't willing to let go. I wasn't willing to own my part in the breakdown, and it was painful. It was almost as heart-wrenching as losing my dad.

I was completely ripped apart, shattered. I dwelt on thoughts of suicide. I never tried, but my thoughts were dangerous. I felt completely trapped and alone, not fully understanding my own feelings or what I had just experienced. Afraid that if I tried to explain to anyone why I was feeling so low, I would lose them, too. I couldn't afford to lose those that had walked with me through tragedy. I cried out to that Voice, and thankfully, He heard me.

Again if I could go back to this day, I'd say:

"He understands. He knows. Your heart will go on. I've seen your heart go to the edge and almost jump off. What you're wrestling with will NOT overcome you or overtake you.

"I know the One who will instantly come to your aid. I've seen the other side. I've seen the whole journey. I wish you could see it.

"The things He will uncover within you—the more you take off the old and embrace the new—will astound you. I've seen the visions He will show you. I've seen the words He will speak to you. I've seen glimpses of the desires He will unearth within you. I've seen how He leads you with indescribable timing, like a father. Never rushing you, just leading you, as you take His hand. All of those things are far more beautiful than anything you have yet experienced. It gets better! So much better!!

"He knows your heart better than you do. Trust Him! Trust Him, and let go. I've seen what He will do (even in spite of your not letting go) and the NEW He walks you into.

"I've seen the mercy He shows you in the face of your own wickedly blind heart! I've seen the forgiveness that will come.

"I bless you with courage. I bless you with comfort. I bless you with encouragement. I bless you with peace. I bless you with clarity. I bless you with fight! I bless the future you, and the freedom that's ahead! I bless this friend with healing. I bless this friend with LIFE!"

Just days after all this blew up, and all the questions came back up, I was asked to speak again. *"What is going to be your response, Jen? What are you going to verbalize to everyone about this Voice who's leading you?"* I spoke about this Voice and how He had provided professionally.

Six months later, we got to enjoy reconciliation and forgiveness, but that fear was still rooted within me, and it was causing havoc! Baby sharks were birthing on more than just my fingertips! My thoughts were waging war with each other and my relationships.

CHAPTER 8

"It Is No Accident You Are Here"

Finding His Voice In The Marketplace/
Entertainment Industry

I was working completely freelance. So, while I had a primary client filling most of my days, I was taking on other projects. I was finally starting to find my rhythm—that is, until the day I got this message on my phone: *"Hey, Jen! There's a movie filming in our city and your favorite superhero is going to be in it! You should go try out!"*

I bet you can't guess what happened next? It was my favorite superhero, after all (have I mentioned I'm a BIG nerd?). I was on a blind date at the time, so naturally...I took him to the audition with me. All this, despite having ZERO interest in ever being an actress. That's normal, right? I just thought it sounded like fun!

No surprise, I was not cast. Neither was my date (of course, he may have had a bigger hill to climb, being a pale redhead and trying out for the role of a Latin soap opera man). But it wasn't a total loss: I ended up with an opportunity to come back as a production assistant (PA).

That little opportunity snowballed. Once they found out I was a designer, I got to help with the entire shoot in the art department. I got to design numerous props and a key four-foot-by-four-foot emblem on the set wall, and I got to enjoy laughing hysterically every day with some new friends.

One new particular friendship started as we were cleaning the set before shooting. During lunch break, she yelled, *"Hey Jen! Fun fact...right where you're sitting I picked up a dead rat!"* Maybe this new friend just had a thing for rodents. One time, while running errands, they told her to break the law to get back in time. Not only did she not break the law, she hit a possum (nah, I'm sure those events are unrelated). But we could have been related with how much we made each other laugh. I laughed so hard, I cried through that entire production.

After seeing my design for the emblem, they asked me to paint it on the wall. I didn't tell them I had never painted before. I was a designer, not a painter. But I paused a second and said, *"It would be my pleasure!"* Of course, I was sweating profusely on the inside. (I'm not the only one who sweats on the inside, right?) I spent an entire weekend alone on the set in preproduction doing JUST that— painting that emblem onto the wall with great detail. I was thrilled by the challenge, and it gave me a new purpose to heal. This opportunity came just weeks after that friend had walked out of my life. I spent that weekend playing music while I painted and cried. It was so healing.

As I painted, the words I had heard my whole life about work swirled within my spirit: ***"work as unto Me, not to men."*** I painted my heart out. The Voice used this moment to change the direction of my life.

As shooting began, I had the time of my life, using my skills on my first feature film. It's definitely not everyday that one of your heroes tells you your painting is dope, that he wants to scrape it off the wall and take it home, or that you end up in a "Harlem Shake" video with the rest of the crew and him flying across the room being carried like Superman. I know, it sounds like the kind of thing that only happens in your weird pizza dreams while you're sleeping, but it would never happen in real life. Well, this kind of thing happens in my real life.

By the end of the shoot, it wasn't the man in tights that had my attention, it was the new friends who felt like family, getting to be with them 24/7, and all the fun we had. Something had come alive within me in a whole new way, right on the heels of another huge loss. I knew that Voice was up to something.

That first film blew me away and opened a lot of doors. It birthed a new pattern: with each production I got hired on, new circles of relationship grew. It became a web that just kept expanding—a web of people that I loved. They stuck everywhere! And I never knew exactly where the next strand was going to go. There was (and is) a randomness to it—kind of like when a friend you haven't seen in years comes up to you and just sticks their finger in your ear. That was how I was feeling every time a seemingly random gig would appear out of "nowhere."

The next web brought me to a shoot in a remote part of the country—think "middle of nowhere in the woods," just to give you some setting. I kept thinking, *"Is this really happening? Is this really my life now?"* I was having the time of my life, while getting to speak LIFE into relationships that were building around me.

My new friend, Todd, is a brilliant composer and lyricist whose words are just as full of wisdom as the music he creates (seriously, he can make music that makes you believe you're listening to the Gladiator, and it's just an indie high school comedy about a spitball war). He summarized the sensation best: ***"It is no accident you are here."*** The moment he said those words, I knew...it's that Voice speaking!

During the shoot, a crewmember received some unexpected bad news about his father. We gathered together and one of the producers turned to me and asked, *"Jen, will you pray for us all?"* I was shocked, as this wasn't a faith-related project by any means. But this producer knew that Voice was important to me and he knew how it had worked in my life.

I said, *"of course!"* We all took time to ourselves to connect with family, if we felt the need, and I went for a walk outside into the woods. As I was walking back, a crew mate stopped me. He had tears in his eyes. He hugged me and thanked me for praying, *"What you said was perfect."* He asked, *"How did you know what to say? As you were praying all I could think was 'What does she have that I don't?'"*

I was flabbergasted. Here I had spent my whole life attending church, and (yes) feeling very out of place at times. I didn't want to work in the nursery, do VBS or things they always want volunteers for. But out here, away from the church, the Voice seemed to be drawing people like a magnet: VOOOMP! Here comes another one!

People became curious about who this Voice was. Later that night, I got question after question about my story, and Todd said, *"for such a time as this, Jen."* Hearts out here are hungry and hurting. Helping these hearts is what drives mine.

+++++

Just as this new season was starting, my family fell apart. New day, new battle. There was so much verbal and emotional abuse, it would have been easy to let it take me down. But I couldn't—not after all the progress I had made. There was a battle being waged for my mind. Things had fallen apart so horribly that the verbal and emotional abuse led me to a place I could easily have been defeated again. I could have believed the lies and gone right off the tracks. The arrows of the enemy cut deeper than I ever would have anticipated, but I knew they were not the Voice.

"No, Jen, I'm right here," the Voice reassured me. *"I will never leave you. Look at all that I am doing!"*

But I'll admit, I felt helpless. No matter what I did, I couldn't seem to win. The more the abuse happened, the more terrified I became. We're talking HOURS of yelling and intense anger, complete rage, even at times when no-one else was even talking. It was as if they weren't even aware of what they were doing. The next day, they didn't seem to remember it even happened.

My family wasn't alone in receiving the rage, and sometimes the rage wasn't even about us. It was just unfocused hostility.

I was so filled with fear that, walking into a family gathering, my entire body shook. One time, I was told not to come home because they were afraid what might happen. Another night, as I heard my mom being yelled at (for hours), I ran and hid in my closet and called a relative on the phone for help. Just the mention that these people might show up to a gathering triggered panic attacks.

But this time, I knew I had to draw the line. There were angry texts and emails. I had to draw more lines. But in the end, my family fell apart. Everyone suffered. We attempted family counseling, but it only made matters worse. I remember sobbing in one session as the abuse continued. Death was spoken over me for the second time in my life. It wasn't a safe place.

Obviously there were a lot of dimensions to the anger and the rage, and I was only one small part of it. But I've since come to realize I did not fully own what I should have in this mess. There was a giant pink elephant in the room, pooping all over the place. No matter what I or anyone else did, we couldn't clean it up. We needed a GIANT pooper-scooper.

One thing I'll forever be grateful for: it taught me to stand up for myself...and my mom! It gave me FIGHT! Not fight with words, but in setting boundaries. It taught me the extremes of forgiveness and grace—for them, but also for myself. Just wait until you hear how that Voice worked, even many years down the road.

If I could go back to this day, I'd say:

"I've seen the other side of this story. Take heart! I've seen what He will do! I've seen the you that's on the other side, where your heart is free. Your heart is BOLD and loud! Your heart is full of forgiveness, both for them, and most importantly, for you.

"Your heart doesn't know what is happening in this season; it's still trapped! But take courage. One day, you will be set free! And YOU will have taken off your own chains. I know your protector is gone, and I see the fear you are in. That Voice has promised He will not leave you helpless! He is your helper. Your warrior is coming. I've seen the words He will use, the humility that will bring restoration, and your shield that is with you! You will win this battle!

"I bless you with courage. I bless you with protection. I bless you with fight! I cancel the death that has been spoken over you, with the authority of that Voice and I send it to the pit! I bless you with LIFE!"

The Voice did not leave me helpless. He spoke through people who loved me; their words were life to me and I clung to them. They gave me the words of LIFE I could speak over my abusers in the midst of the pain. That Voice ARMED me, filled my sack with artillery, and made me feel like Wonder Woman.

He spoke through friends and coworkers, without them even knowing it at the time. They just spontaneously spilled forth love for me.

One time, a friend sent me an email reminding me of how present He was, how seen I was, and important I was to Him. So I continued on, confident that He was with me.

CHAPTER 9

"I've Still Got You"

The Web Expands

Soon, another production opportunity emerged. Before the gig even started, as I was questioning whether or not I was going to do it, The Voice spoke distinctly and softly: ***"Take courage and trust me, Jen".***

So I did.

Once again, I fell in love with working on set, and the people I was with. It's a strange feeling when you're averaging about 3-4 hours of sleep per night and cannot wait to get back to set the next morning. I loved everyone I was meeting. We got to spend so much time together, sharing all our meals, as well as the holidays, and working late into the night. It started to feel like a family—one that had come together from all different parts of the country. Each person brought their own personality, culture, and nuances in tow. Every day was like a treasure waiting to be found.

There was an elderly woman (a cast member), who could never remember what she was supposed to wear, but when it came to sticking peas in her ears for a Thanksgiving scene, she excelled, shoving in a whole bowl-full.

I'll never forget how this production ended. At the end, we learned why the script had been written, which brought me to tears. I knew it was no mistake I had been there. It was written by a man who grew up going to church, but had been so bullied in college that he tried to commit suicide. At that moment, his life changed. He discovered that, no matter what you agreed or disagreed with in life, the key to a good life was to love people first. Listening to his story, I had chills. It was exactly what I had been given: the chance to work on yet another gig, and show that love to so many new friends. It was a message I felt deep in my core, and I might have missed it, had I not *"taken courage, and trusted"* that Voice to shape and lead my heart. Every single person matters, and how you treat them means everything. It's a matter of life and death. This voice was continuing to open my eyes to the hearts of those around me—all the hearts. That passion inside of me glowed brighter.

If I could go back to this day, I'd say:

"Yes, Jen!!! This is so huge! I know you see the power of the message as it's hitting you. You see the hearts around you. But you don't know the full power behind what this moment and this message will do for your own journey and your story. I've seen the day this message will ring so loud within your own soul, it will set YOU free! You will watch another courageous heart share their pain, their journey, and inspire thousands of others to too be set free. That heart—that story—will be the one that brings the whole house down.

"I bless the heart for others that is building within you. I bless the authentic eyes with which you view the world. I bless the continued journey with wisdom, discernment until you reach that day. I bless the future you, with freedom and power as you help others, feel seen!"

+++++

The film industry became a deep rabbit hole for me. After the experience with the superhero, the shoot in the middle of nowhere, and the elderly woman with peas in her ears, relationships grew and opportunities abounded. The months were filled with adventure, bringing not only production work, but pre-production and post-production opportunities, too.

The words from that Voice, ***"Don't put off until tomorrow what you can do today,"*** was swimming laps in my brain. I decided to enroll in film school for continued education. I had been getting all these gigs, but had never had any training in film. Design, sure, but not film. I thought it might be wise to learn what all the other people I was working with did. I figured it would make me more valuable at future gigs. That Voice was right there with me, reassuring me that, if I were meant to do this and juggle all life was dealing, He'd give me floaties. I mean, all the children wear them and they seem to be fine.

Like a Father, that Voice knew what I needed to hear, and when. A professor randomly said one day during class, *"I can just sense it, Jen's going to be an award-winning Art Director someday."* I laughed, after all it's not at all embarrassing to be called out in the middle of class, is it (winky smile)? But in reality, I needed a line of encouragement that day. Whether she meant it seriously or not, I was sure that Voice had seen me that day and I felt more confident there was a future waiting for me.

That wasn't all that Voice had been up to. I may be

wrong, but I absolutely think He had quite a sense of humor, and knew how much I liked to laugh.

Just before I worked on that first feature film, I attended a comic book convention in Chicago. But I didn't just attend; I was completely decked out as Wonder Woman. I was a BIG nerd. I can prove it: one year, I attended with my entire body painted blue (you know, like an Avatar) and I painted three of my friends blue, too. That was fun (especially painting the one who didn't know we were going to be painting them blue—we just showed up blue and said, *"Hey we gotta paint you"*).

Dressed as Wonder Woman that second year, I stepped onto an elevator and who stepped onto the elevator with me? Dean Cain—Superman from the TV show, *"Lois & Clark, the New Adventures of Superman."* He gave me a nod and said, "nice costume." Four years later, I got a chance to work with him, and I assure you I absolutely never mentioned our previous meeting. I was so embarrassed, and prayed my costume had disguised my inner EPIC nerd. I wanted him to view me as a normal person!

Never saw that coming.

That same day I rode the elevator with Superman, I rode the elevator with another famous star known for

his Herculean strength (you guessed it: Kevin Sorbo).
A year-and-a-half after the first film experience, I got to
work with Mr. Sorbo. Again, I chose not to mention our
previous meeting, I just chuckled at the Voice and said,
"you got me." I definitely did not want to be known as
the major nerd on set (even if it was totally true). I got to
create a handful of specialty hero props for the film, which
was super fun.

You bet I was careful from this point forward who I
rode on elevators with while being a nerd. I learned you
never know whom you might ride with.

+++++

Before the next production could take off, another
loss hit: my grandma passed away (grandpa had passed a
few years prior from cancer). They had been like second
parents to me. Not only did I grow up with them only 5
minutes away, but our entire extended family spent every
single Sunday afternoon at their house, and we spent every
holiday with them. As they got older, they were less able
to care for themselves and spent their latter years literally
downstairs from me. I grew up with grandparents that
not only loved me, but also believed in me and celebrated
every single time I shared another design project I was
working on, or news of things that had happened. They
loved relentlessly, with all that they had.

I'll always remember the words my composer friend, Todd shared with me at that time: *"We don't live to remove scars; we learn how to live with them. Just as the wound that caused them was deeper than the skin on the surface, there can be a peace that runs even deeper. Sometimes that peace cannot be found without a deep would that makes it a necessity; like a tree growing deeper roots because there is no water."*

The heavy emotions from the past came back strong, but my roots were animating, plus there was that Voice again: ***"Jen...I've still got you...and I'm going to WOW you yet again."*** While there's not a day I didn't wish dad back, I was so thankful for the roots He cultivated in me. The Voice walked with me through another loss, and I found a new kind of peace through it. I didn't know what the future held, but I felt like anything was possible.

That Voice kept speaking to me about who He was... and who I am. Sometimes He spoke through people, other times it was just a sense. So many times, I felt overwhelmed by the weight of my family's issues. I wanted to share all these changes in my life with my dad, my grandpa, and grandma—all the "big" moments of life. The Voice was speaking right into my needs and met every one. I found myself pressing forward in a kind of trust, and I felt an overwhelming reassurance that this Voice was taking care of me. As the roller coaster of emotions hit, I felt empowered that life was not meant to be wasted, but to be lived!

Again, if I could go back to this day, I'd say:

"Yes, Jen!!! That Voice is continuing to show you with every loss that HE IS WITH YOU, allowing perseverance to build. He is increasing your vision for what's ahead and building a pep in your step from the LIFE He is building within you. He will finish what He started!

"You are a warrior training for battle and your armor is being layered on. Piece by piece, He is preparing you for an epic win! Keep fighting! Keep listening for Him, listening for that still, subtle Voice, as He continues to lead His warrior to greatness!

"You are the warrior He will use to lead others to greatness! You will fight for the broken. Fight for the hurting. Uniting the wounded around the world as they become free, prepare for future battles, and win even bigger ones!"

+++++

As the next gig started, that Voice was back, swimming laps in my head: *"don't put off until tomorrow what you can do today."* It was a timely message, as I received my first opportunity to head up the whole art department as Production Designer for a film, including wardrobe, set design/dressing, props, graphics, and much more. Oh snap! I'd never done that before. But sure...ummm...I can do that!

I had a lot of conversations with that Voice, asking Him to go before me, saying, *"there's no WAY I can do this without you!"* And I surely couldn't have. We spent over six months prepping the art direction for the whole department, plus all the pre-production graphic and specialty prop needs. But I was beyond excited to be back working with many of my film friends.

The Voice, the Holy Composer I knew by this point, was at the helm, steering the ship for all that life held. (Aye, Aye, Captain! This is quite the storm. What say we find the rum? Or maybe just a pretty palm tree to sit under and soak up a tan? Who am I kidding? I don't tan. Translucent people don't tan; they burn.) Well, I didn't find the rum or sit under a palm tree, but I did start to ask the terrible question: *"Is this really what I'm suppose to be doing?"* Would you believe I found an answer? I really found something.

This particular production had a tiny little micro-budget—I mean barely ANY budget—so I was digging through all the crap in our basement to find materials, trying to be as resourceful as I could. Deep within the labyrinth of storage boxes, I found a dusty trove of picture frames and started stripping out the contents. One particular frame contained a long-forgotten photo with a cryptic message on the back, that ended with this phrase:

"This is the way, walk ye in it."

Flabbergasted once again at how direct He had been with me, addressing my doubts, I felt a sudden peace rush over me. To know you're going the right direction is a surprisingly refreshing sensation. It's like a tall glass of a lemonade in a musty storage closet. I continued making myself available for whatever each day held; I was totally present for it. I knew each day, each minute, had a purpose.

How did I know this? Before this production began, I had a quick visit to Los Angeles with my film school. While I was there, the producer of the film I was about to work on randomly texted me: *"No way! You're there too?"* We made plans to meet up and attend a worship event in downtown Hollywood. After the service, we went out to coffee with a few new friends we had made.

I chatted with another woman who had also come to the event for the first time. She shared that her sister had recently committed suicide. She went on to quote the words that had come to mean so much to her: *"I will never leave you or forsake you."* Did I mention that I have that tattooed on my arm? I looked at her in shock, held out my forearm, and said, *"read the tattoo on my arm."* We swapped stories and tears as we shared how amazing that Voice had been in both of our lives. That Voice was continuing to show me how powerfully present He was all around me.

After the trip to Los Angeles, we were up to our eyeballs, getting ready for the film. Only the guidance of the Voice got me through. It was a thrilling experience, but as the Production Designer for the first time, I knew going into it that He would have to do something major to get it all done. He did just that. My spoken and unspoken needs were met in tremendous ways, and I was constantly reminded how much that Voice was at work behind the scenes.

One evening, as the production wrapped up, the Producer exclaimed, *"I really think the strongest part of the entire production has been the art department."* I teared up. What a moment for me! And a confirmation. We were setting a location for another scene near where a band was rehearsing. *"You make all things work together for my good,"* boomed from their voices. I looked to the sky, pointed, and exclaimed, *"This is all you."* That Voice had become quite the poet with how He was weaving His words within each moment.

131

There were so many affirming remarks from the crew, but I believe that's because my heart was completely in it. One time, as a cast member was laying face-down in the mud for a scene, she had a hair in her mouth. I scraped her tongue with my hand to get it out for her, several times. It's what I do. She exclaimed *"You're the best Jen"*.

Before that year was over, we squeezed in another small project—another opportunity for the Voice to tickle my funny bone. An actress who had appeared in the James Bond film series was cast as a lead. This was quite an ironic nudge for a girl who at that time drove a car with the license plate MNYPNNY (in honor of the secretary, Ms. Moneypenny, in the James Bond films). I didn't want to be a Bond girl, I wanted to be the secretary, simply for the fact that it would make people laugh who saw it. Don't tell her though (my car), because I left her (my car) behind on that production. I haven't had the heart to tell her.

I think she knows.

CHAPTER 10

"Be Watchful"

Expecting Miracles

I continued to work on a lot of gigs for the same company that made me the art lead; they even brought me in to help do graphics for their non-profit. As it turns out, this producer was also a pastor. Relationships blossomed for me with their community, like flowers popping up everywhere! I traveled to conferences with them, even all the way to Hawaii. As I did, that Voice led me further. The first trip to Hawaii was so powerful, I walked away with a new vigor for what the Voice had been doing in my life. That Voice, the relationships I cared about, and my new home industry were pumping through my veins.

I began to start each day by talking to that Voice about

those people I cared so much for by name. There were so many people who had done so much to bring about healing in me, whether they meant to or not. I wanted to do something in return, and this was the only response that felt right.

One friend I hadn't seen for a long time kept coming up in my heart, so I called her and we planned to meet. She was late, so she called me to say *"I'm sorry I'm late...I got held up talking to my grandma about religion!"* I was shocked that our catch-up started out right away referencing the Voice, especially for someone who had been unsure it even existed! As we talked about her struggle, the conversation kept coming back to that Voice.

Suddenly, she exclaimed, *"I felt like He was saying, 'See...you really do need me, you can't do this on your own.'"* I was so blown away by how vivid this Voice had been communicating, not only with me, but with this friend I had been praying for—and here was proof that He was responding. This Voice wasn't just working in me and speaking to me, it was continuing to speak to those around me.

Now that I could see that He talks to and listens to me, I started thinking, *"There's something to that!!"* I started going into EVERYTHING by first seeking and talking to it beforehand. On my way to meet the producers of the next film at a local coffee shop, I pulled over to the side of the road and talked to that Voice. And guess what? He went with me! Not only did that Voice wow me in the meeting, but I'll never forget what happened during that production.

I had prayed that this Voice would be so evident in the process of the production that it would just radiate how present it/He was. I wanted others—people I cared about—to experience how amazing He was! And by "others," I mean everyone I met!

I had been getting to know the main department heads on this production. One woman in particular was in the midst of a huge change in her life after working in Las Vegas for 12 years as a dancer.

The moment I met Elissa, I was stunned by her beauty, her commanding presence, and powerful heart. She had the most striking eyes, eyes that made you feel like you had her complete attention when you spoke to her, that you mattered and were important. I noticed very quickly that it wasn't just me she treated this way; it was everyone, even strangers. She had an amazing gift to simply see everyone around her. But as I looked into those eyes, I could also see a heart that ached to be deeply seen in return. It was obvious to me that she didn't see the powerful woman I saw.

The director went to church with me and then out to lunch. As we talked about the film we were about to shoot and got to know each other, I felt led to mention to him (just in case it would be helpful) that I could personally speak to the journey that the main character goes through. I wasn't trying to "tell my story" to him, but rather meant to let him know that I might be able to help him process through that character's emotions. The main character tragically lost her dad, and has to face her fears of "losing" several others until she hears a "supernatural" character trying to whisper to her.

WHAAAAAAAAAAAAT?!?! Am I getting 'punked?!?! I wasn't; this was really happening. Danny Trejo was also cast as this supernatural character, pretty crazy for a name who usually wielded a machete in his roles. The director was so shocked that he pulled out his phone immediately and recorded the rest of our conversation. For the next hour, I shared my journey and answered his questions about my experience with the Voice. We both were blown as we realized the depth of the story we had on our hands. It just seemed like the team had been brought together—dare I say it—supernaturally. We had such a powerful time together.

About 20 minutes after we parted, Elissa called and said, *"Jen!! I just walked into the hotel and heard about your crazy lunch and how cool that is!! It's like I've told you already...it's like the people who are here are meant to be here.*" I was almost in tears. After asking that Voice to be evident, here we were in pre-production—still a week away from shooting—and this new friend who's trying to change her life sees the Voice at work.

If I could go back to this day I'd say:

"Yes Jen!!! Something NEW has birthed. Something powerful. Not only in the intentionality with which you are seeking that Voice BEFORE you step into things, but in what it's doing in the lives of those around you! Something NEW has birthed within you, and within this new friend.

"Remember this moment. Remember this feeling. I see the war still ahead of both of you. I know every heartache, every prayer, every moment you will get on your knees and fight for this new friend. I know all the words both you and that Voice will yet speak into this heart. I see you pouring into others. I see the tears, the days you question all your efforts! But I also see what comes of it. I see the day you look back with gratitude for all that Voice has done for this friend, admiration for how free and powerful this friend has become! You saw it on Day One. What you see, He sees, and He will finish what He has begun!

"I bless your heart for others. I bless this friend's heart and journey with continued freedom-more freedom than she ever dreamed. I bless this friend with power! I bless this friend with LIFE! I bless this friend with a future so bright, it radiates and breaks the darkness!"

That film experience was mind-boggling. Not only did that Voice do a mic-drop in preproduction, but in designing the sets, that Voice guided me into things I couldn't have come up with on my own. I even had to represent Him in the design of one, but how do you represent that Voice?!?! It had been speaking to me ever since tragedy hit, so I knew exactly what to do. I saw the whole thing in my head, and boy, did we have fun! That set was one of the RICHEST sets I ever designed, there was so much depth to it, so many layers. So many hidden treasures. The set itself was like going down a rabbit hole. It made you ask questions as you looked about the room.

- What's that over there?
- What ya got under there?
- What does this mean?
- You're up to something aren't you?

It piqued your curiosity. Never once giving the answer, just making you want to know more. When it came time to shoot a scene on this set the writer of the book the film was based on came over to me and said, *"Are you the one responsible for this?! Did you do this?"* He gave me a huge hug and started to cry: *"This is EXACTLY what I envisioned in writing the book! THANK YOU!!"* Tears filled my eyes too, it meant so much to me to get this one right. To get that Voice right.

The Voice was reaching well beyond that room. I was making new friends. Elissa and I went to grab a beer at the bar and swap stories. Suddenly, in the middle of a sentence she grabbed my knee, looked me dead in the eyes, and said, *"Jen, I haven't let anyone talk to me about that Voice in over 12 years."* Needless to say, a powerful friendship started during this production, and that Voice continued to work through it.

I sensed the Voice asking me: ***"Are you afraid to ask God to do big things in your life? Abandon your doubts, reclaim your faith: faith in yourself, faith in your abilities, and faith in your future. Faith in that Voice! He specializes in the things thought impossible. And make no mistake, He can help you do things you never dreamed possible...your job is to let Him, instead of doubting His power. Trust Him! Expect Him to work miracles, and be watchful!".***

Watchful, I was.

CHAPTER 11

"Ask Her, Her Story"

Another Hurting Heart

January ushered in a new year with a bang and a new adventure (not a real bang; I don't travel by canon—I hopped on a plane). I was off to London. Had applied for a two-week intensive training in Production Design at the London Film School, where only nine seats were available. I was so honored to be accepted.

Have you ever heard of a curriculum vitae (CV)? Ok cool, neither had I. But I had to learn what it was FAST and get it submitted in order for them to consider me. For those who don't know it's an EXPANSIVE resume: pages and pages, proving who you are and why you should be allowed. Yuuuuuck. But oh, was it worth it.

I had the time of my life, meeting other production designers from around the world, while we spent two weeks learning from some of the greatest! My classmates were from all over; Chile, Argentina, Uruguay, Mexico, Canada, and the UK! It was incredible! Sure, I had to travel alone to Europe, and figure out how I was going to stay in London all by myself for the experience, but that ended up being a blast! I may have had my fears on the way, but it was worth it! And I knew, everyday, that Voice was with me, everywhere I went.

And of course, you can't go to London and not visit the other parts of Europe, right? I mean, everything's so close! So after the course was over, Elissa flew over and we traveled through Europe together. We hit up more of London, Ireland, Paris, and Berlin, before returning home.

If I could go back to this day, I'd say:

"Yes Jen!!! You just showed so much courage, and trust in that Voice. That Voice was with you every step of the way! Keep trusting it in every moment. I've seen the journeys and adventures He continues to take you on. I've seen your courage grow beyond your travels. He is doing a NEW thing in you. And this is not all that he wants to show you; there is so much more! Trust that still, small, subtle Voice. He will be with you wherever you go!"

Even things at home changed. I said this new year started with a bang. Well, the bang wasn't over. Once we got home from Europe, I packed up my entire life in Michigan and moved across the country to Las Vegas! I had never been there; never even had a desire to visit. But at that point in my life, why not? I was in my thirties, single, and I wanted to see what else that Voice had for me. I knew that all the opportunities in my life were because of personal relationships I had built with people—all the gigs I was getting were coming because of making friends—and I knew that the opportunities in the Midwest were limited. I could see the roof and I wanted to go higher!

I knew that, if I wanted to continue to see what this life had, I needed to develop more relationships on the other side of the country. I took the first opportunity that came. Elissa needed a roommate, so I moved in (we don't need to talk about the fact that it took me five days to get there.)

+++++

That next year was full of excitement, but also a lot of hardship. As I got opportunities to do some of the coolest things, that Voice really had to go to work. I was stretched in so many ways I hadn't been stretched before. But it was so good for me. I learned so much and had to lean even more into that Voice.

If you've never been to Nevada, it is mostly mountains and valleys, which is exactly how my life felt. My work felt like mountains. But my home life was becoming a deep valley. I quickly realized the environment I had moved into was not stable, and things I had intentionally chosen never to be around were suddenly in my home.

I deeply loved Elissa, and often spoke life over her, but our lives could not have been more opposite. What started as a healthy friendship soon spiraled into conflict. Don't get me wrong, I was at fault for some of it, but at other times I often felt helpless. Every morning I was on my knees, in my closet, in battle for this friend's heart, my own, and our environment. I came to find out later how hard the Voice was working to keep me safe that full first year.

Don't get me wrong, I freaking love her to this day, and our friendship has completely changed. But at that season, living together was hard—and a big part of the reason it was so hard was my fault.

But through it all, that Voice was not only working in this friend's life, but in mine, too. He was leading us both through the whole thing, with crumbs of a trail that would lead not only her to freedom, but me too. I couldn't be more proud of who I saw her become over time: a powerhouse with a heart for others. I saw it on Day One;

eventually she saw it too! She became a leader for her family and a cheerleader in my life. She believed in me more vocally than most ever had.

The Las Vegas Strip is one of those places everyone should experience once, even if they hate that kind of thing (like me). I was in total overload when I attended the Billboards Awards that year, so I was excited to go back for a hockey game later in the year. We walked what felt like the entire Strip—both to and from the game—to get to our car, and enjoyed dinner on the Strip after the game, sitting outdoors in view of it all.

As we pulled into the driveway at home, we heard the news: there had been a massive shooting at the Mandalay Bay Resort. We had missed being in the middle of it by minutes. As the rest of the nation watched this horrific event unfold all over the news, we knew it had almost been us. We saw the city band together in the most beautiful way.

+++++

One evening, I got a call from a frantic producer asking if I could jump in and help with a project over the next two days. I was desperate for work and said yes to help art direct, but had no context for what we were even going to be doing. I was just told to show up the next day. What could go wrong, riiiiiight?

A few hours into the gig, I started to get frustrated because I didn't understand why they even needed me. I was sent on runs for sandwiches(!), even though I'd been hired to help with art. Surely they didn't call me because they were having trouble deciding between ham and turkey?!

As I started asking that Voice why I was there, it became apparent. As I was waiting for everyone to arrive at the next locale, in walked our lead. All I knew up to that point was that it was a documentary / interview-style project about someone. Paloma walked in and sat down on the couch across from me. The Voice that had been talking to me my whole life nudges me, ***"Ask her her story, Jen."***

Ok sure, but it'd be rude to yell that from way over here. I walked over, introduced myself and said, *"I'm so sorry, I know we're interviewing you today, but I don't know why. Would you mind sharing with me your story, I would love to hear it if you're willing?"*

She was willing. She spent the next 20 minutes sharing her heart while we waited for the rest of the crew. Tears streamed down Paloma's face, her voice shook, and as she grabbed my leg in sharing what had been a horrific day, I learned Paloma had been there in the midst of the shooting in our city. She had saved a man's life. She had been driving for a car company and was downtown when the shots rang out, and a Voice—one that I now believe was the same one that had been talking to me—told her, ***"go back down there."*** She obeyed the direction, and as she arriving in the chaos, a man frantically jumped into the back of her moving vehicle. This man had been shot in the side and the bullet had come out the other side. He was bleeding out. She raced to the hospital and prayed fiercely. An inexplicable peace came over the car as they pulled up to the hospital. That was the last thing she knew. Since that day, she has struggled with PTSD. She shared with me how it affected her family and her spirit.

I asked her, *"this Voice you spoke of…are you a woman of faith?"* She responded, *"sort of."* I knew my time with this woman was going to be limited, and that at any minute they might call her for the next scene, so I asked her, *"before these two days are over, would it be ok if I prayed over you?"*

With tears in her eyes, she gripped my leg and said, *"I would LOVE that!"*

The rest of our time together, I learned the rest of her story, and I was blown away by what I saw. On the second day, the crew gathered inside of a home to shoot another scene, we got wind of a surprise that was brewing: imagine the celebration as she reunited with the man whose life she had saved! There was not a dry eye in the place. Witnessing this man share, *"my kids still have a father because of you,"* is a moment I'll never forget. As a woman whose heart PUMPED for people…wow, I knew in that moment that Voice had brought me here.

If I could perfectly describe the kinds of gigs I hoped to work on or be a part of someday, this would be exactly it. This gig was about people and their amazing stories of life—the very stories that saved a life.

At the end of this short shoot was a scene set at a gas station. Paloma made her rounds, thanking the crew with hugs and heartfelt tears. I couldn't wait to hug her. As she embraced me, she wept and said, *"Jen, thank you so much for ASKING me my story. Not only could I tell that you truly wanted to know, but I could tell you really cared. That moment meant everything to me, and even in that brought even more healing."*

The truth is, I really did care; I cared deeply. In our few short moments, she felt it. I took this last fleeting opportunity to pray for her. I think it meant as much to me as it did to her.

CHAPTER 12

"You Are Home"

On The Edge

At this point, you're probably thinking, *"Man Jen, you must have been through the roof overjoyed with where this Voice led you, especially with your heart for people."* Like the day when a crewmember was laying completely flat on the floor during our lunch break, I tossed a gummy bear at her, and it bounced off her chest and directly into her mouth. As shocked as I was, imagine how she felt, since she didn't know it was coming until it was in her mouth! That was fun, but my joy went deeper than moments like that.

At the same time, I couldn't have been more frustrated as the next few months passed by. I was beyond frustrated.

Sure, I had prayed for Paloma. This couldn't be all I could offer this woman, could it? This woman needed more than just prayer! I stewed over it. As I thought about all the paths I had crossed in 14 years—all the moments I had shared with people—they couldn't have been just coincidences, just nice moments. It gnawed at me. My heart was completely wrenched. I was heavy for an answer; heavy for more. There had to be more. And to be frank, I was desperate for an answer.

Little did I know how desperate that next year would become. I had to find it. I could feel myself coming to an edge. Another January rolled around and I felt like I was falling backward to that dark place of feeling shattered and suicidal.

I was getting ready to leave in the morning for a conference I had been invited to, but in this dark moment I found myself at a crossroads. I could go back to the dark place I had been or I could go forward into this new opportunity.

Suddenly, I found myself in a new place. The fog was lifting and I found myself redirected. I was sitting in a business conference that had been recommended to me by a friend. In one day, I went from the dark road of despair to life. Just like that. I was desperate for life, and I found it. I was on my way to *First Steps To Success* with Dani

Johnson.

Remember that woman I spoke of in Chapter 1? We're coming full circle; the bomb is about to go off. Could this really be what I thought it was?! Could this Voice literally be leading me to the very LIFE my heart had been crying for...the very weekend I was about to drive it straight toward its death?

That's exactly what I believe happened. January 19, 2018 is one of those pivotal dates that resets a life. Have you ever been so completely shocked and stunned that it was like someone took a defibrillator to your heart and jolted you back to life, and you woke up with a ZEST for it that you didn't even know you needed? Well, I got defibrillator (I'm sure that's not a word).

It's like being at a hockey game with a friend and as this friend exclaims, *"I don't really know what to do with my life, I feel like it will one day just hit me."* And then they get hit by the hockey puck in the face. It was like that. Totally.

I was smack dab in the front row of hundreds of people listening to one of the most engaging, stunningly beautiful, powerful, successful, authentic, and genuine hearts I had ever witnessed. I'm serious; I'm not just saying nice things.

Have you ever attended a conference where someone drones on and on and you can barely stay awake, let alone stay engaged? You get ambushed by a daydream sneak attack.

Boom! There's Puff the Magic Dragon again.

And now we're singing.

Stop singing. No one else is singing. You're in a conference.

Oh, right.

This woman was so engaging, NONE of that happened, and I stayed engaged for over nine hours in one day!!! I didn't want to miss a single word she said.

WHAT THE HECK IS HAPPENING TO ME?!

You might also think I'm crazy for sitting in the front row at a conference by a woman I had never even heard of. Well, I did feel crazy…in the beginning. But remember, I was desperate.

I was there on the recommendation of a friend I had met in the film industry. When he said, *"I know this sounds crazy, but I have someone who you can be a line buddy with, but he likes to get up early, so you'd have to get in line at 2 or 4 am and then swap with him."*

Wait, what? Are you serious? People get in line this early? Who is this woman!? What's a line buddy? Are they going to try to hold my hand?!

Despite thinking that was absolutely nuts for a few seconds, I responded, *"Heck, let's do it! If I'm going to do this, whatever it is…I'm all-in! I'll do it!"* Little did I know how pivotal it would be. That very response would shape the entire rest of my year, and maybe the rest of my life.

How many times that weekend did I exclaim, "Who is this woman?!" It was like seeing Danielle sitting next to me. Obviously you don't know Danielle. I met Danielle early that morning waiting in line in pajamas with her hair up and no makeup on, and here she was again, but elegantly dressed with beautiful hair and makeup, and I didn't recognize her when she asked me to go to lunch. Please forgive me now, in case I ever unknowingly do this to you. People look different when they're in their pajamas than when they are all glammed up for a business conference…very different. And let's be honest: everyday, I say to the woman I see staring back at me in the mirror, *"Who dat?!!!"* I mean, come on, have you seen my hair? Well, that's not what it looks like all funked up in the morning after tossing and turning for eight hours. I'm a very restless sleeper.

The entire weekend felt completely surreal. I was

overwhelmed by how much I felt sure the Voice had heard the cries of my heart for 14 years. After so much frustration and torment, I felt like I was released from whatever was holding me back from believing in big dreams and a big God the way I always wanted to. I felt free to love people again. I knew the Voice was way bigger still. I felt vision rise up again. I saw the path He had been leading me on. I couldn't have ever imagined the life He had been giving me those 14 years. My heart knew it had a specific purpose, and a passion for people; hurting, lonely, and broken people. I had a message for them, filled with stories from my journey—the ones I've been sharing with you! It was a big day for my heart!

That weekend, I knew I was listening to the leader my heart had been silently aching for my entire life. Have you ever felt like you have unspoken cries deep within your soul that you don't even think anyone ever hears or could even handle answering? I did. Many had never been voiced; I surely didn't think anyone listened to them (I do now). Up until that point, I had never met any leader who thought big enough for my dreams, and had the track record to back it up. I had that Voice, who had already done so much, but I knew there was more available. I knew that He had more for me. Do you know that Voice can hear your heart? I truly believe it can now, with what I've seen it do.

Up until that point, people thought, and even said to me, *"We can't believe what that Voice has done in your life after tragedy!!"* Honestly, I couldn't believe it either. But no one knew how to answer the big question: where the heck I go from here? This can't be all there is! As great as the story seemed at times, I was still completely broke, frustrated with my dreams and still broken more deeply than I knew. But that was all changing.

So, let's get real. Why was I frustrated? Sure, I was broke, but how could I be frustrated when my referrals were flourishing and the relationships I was building with broken crew friends were continuing after every film?! Wasn't that my dream? Wasn't it the pang of my heart to speak life into hurting, broken, and lonely hearts? What was my deal?

Well, for one, I didn't know it until that weekend, but I had been letting other voices tell me that I wasn't successful. Those other voices said that, unless I was booking films back-to-back, I was failing. I knew the vision and passion the Voice had placed on my heart, and He was literally giving it to me every time I booked a gig... and yet I believed I was failing!!

I left every gig with new friends who were like family, and I was pouring into them because I knew they were loved and meant for more. Still, I was telling myself that I was failing!!

The moment I realized this, I had tears in my eyes. It took this leader—this courageous heart on stage—to hit me over the head with it! It took a leader who listened to that same Voice and a place where I felt the presence of that Voice from the instant I arrived. I sensed it through Dani and everyone there. It took a leader who believed in big dreams and a big God, and was living it, teaching it, and wanted it for other people.

The cry of my heart was answered, and I saw myself in her those first two days. I saw a leader I wanted to follow. I couldn't have been more excited to run faster and dream even higher and bigger. She showed me how. She saw me and every single other face in that room. I saw all that in an instant. It was like time stood still.

Then there was the incredible moment where this leader stopped in the middle of speaking, looked right at me, stuck out her hand, and said, *"Hi, I'm Dani."* I shook her hand and out stumbled, *"Hi, I'm Jen"*. In the middle of speaking!! In that moment, I truly believe that Voice knew I needed that and prompted her to stop—in the middle of everything—and welcome me. That it was important and she listened to that direction.

That moment showed me that this leader was different,

that these people were different. It wasn't going to be just another conference where I made a few new friends or picked up some awesome takeaways that changed my life.

THIS...this was something different.

I saw all of that in that one gesture.

I needed it right then, and the Voice knew it: ***"Don't let the excuse of what happened to you, and the absence of your dad, ever let you think for one second that you don't STILL have a family! I've brought you family in every season and I'm NOT going to stop teaching it to you now. You are home."***

That Voice had given me many amazing teams of influencers and family over the years, but not "The One" yet, the leader who dreamed big enough for my dreams. January 2018, that Voice led me to her.

As I prepared to leave that conference, that Voice still had more to say. As I was chatting with a few new friends on the way out, a woman from South Africa named Linda walked up to me, placed her hands on my shoulders, and said ***"I know we only had a few minutes together, but I can tell that you've been through a lot. And do you know that He (the Voice) sees every tear we have cried? I can sense that's been a lot for you. He also says that He keeps every single one of the tears that we cry, and he keeps them in*** *a vial...and He promises to bless us far more than the amount of tears that we've cried. I can't wait to see what He does with you, because I know it's going to be huge."*

WHAT?!

This woman didn't know my story; she knew nothing about me other than my name and what I did for a living. How could she see THAT?

In that moment, it was more than just her—it was Him. It was that Voice reassuring me that He was there, not letting me leave without a huge message of hope.

The next morning, as I awaited my flight, I called my mom to catch up from the weekend. The moment she picked up the phone, I just burst into tears. No words could even come out. I knew as soon as they did, she'd know how huge this weekend had been for me. Little did I know how huge it really was. What I was about to embark on was a journey that far exceeded even the epic-ness of that weekend. It wasn't just the Voice—it was like rivers of the Voice.

Again if I could go back, I'd say:

"Everything you're feeling is SPOT ON! Trust what that Voice is confirming within you and around you. Trust the Voice that led you here. Trust

the experience He just led you through and what he's led you to. This is just the beginning.

"I know the road that's still ahead of you. I know what awaits you. I know the things this Voice will yet say to you, show you, and lead you to! I know what you will overcome! I've seen the person that you will become. If you could see her, there is NOTHING that would stop you from getting there. No matter what, press on! Fight! Embrace every moment and every battle with everything you've got.

"He is with you! He is not done with you! You were born with the gift of FAITH! Have faith that what He is doing He will continue to do! I bless you with more faith. I bless you with courage. I bless you with trust! I bless you with an unwavering spirit that runs after the life you see so close within your reach!"

CHAPTER 13

"Here For A Reason"

Going All-In

So now, you might be thinking, "*Okay, we get it, Jen. That first conference was crazy impactful for you. But what did you actually learn?!*"

I learned a whole heck of a lot, and with what I learned—and then applied—I saw massive results almost immediately. I was desperate, so I HAD to apply it. I HAD to have change in my life. I HAD to see if what I was learning actually worked! I HAD to see if the success stories around me were true. It was either that or I would stay completely broke, beyond frustrated, heading down a track to more brokenness, thoughts of suicide, and maybe even my death. Definitely the death of a huge dream. I

HAD to see if this worked.

I took massive action almost immediately. I bought the recordings of the event and wore them out. I scoured my notes for details until the ink faded. The biggest result came in just two days. I got hired to work on a music video for an A-lister! NOT because there was even a position open for me, but because I used a skill I learned at the conference. A friend who was on the gig paid money out of his own pocket to have me come work for him. He CREATED a position for me!

Up until that point in my life, I had always dreamed of working at that level of production, but had never reached it. I giddily geeked out in anticipation of the day I would GET to work on something that creative, and here I was! As I'm sitting here writing this, that music video now has well over 59 million views.

While at the shoot, I ended up in a situation where another younger crewmember started asking me questions about the Voice.

I could just leave it at that, and I'm sure that result would speak for itself, but that's not all that happened in that first month after the conference. That gig led to the next one, as that same contact then hired me to work in the art department on a foreign film—my first foreign project! With how broke I had been up to that point in my life, I was astounded: that one gig paid more than I had made in half a month…in just one week. And we didn't just shoot for one week, we shot for a month and a half. I worked my tail off, using skills and tools I had learned at the conference (alongside the skills I already knew). I worked with excellence, and got paid well for it. I worked with honor, and took it to a whole new level, thanks to my new coach.

I also worked with Chinese translators, because I absolutely had no idea how to read or speak Chinese.

Soon after, five more production gig leads sprouted. Leads came in for feature films in Mississippi, Pennsylvania, Nevada, Michigan, Colorado, and even Germany—all for various roles, and timelines, but all as either a member or leader of the art department.

I remember one Sunday dinner gathering with my amazing and quirky extended family, when the 15 of us were eating and I suddenly got hit in the chest by a dog toy, in the forehead by a nerf bullet, and then three bags of lettuce, for no other reason than to say with their actions, *"Hey you, we love ya!"* They knew my humor, but they also knew I loved them. That's why I showed up to one of their Thanksgiving gatherings in a turkey costume, and a Christmas party dressed as an oddball character from "Saturday Night Live" who had baby-sized hands. Opening presents was hard, but they knew I loved them in that strange moment.

Point being, just as I was bombarded with a dog toy, nerf bullet, and bags of lettuce, I was bombarded with gigs. I felt so loved by that Voice.

+++++

With every lead, even the calls themselves changed powerfully. I felt free and empowered to engage the lead in the way my heart preferred to: valuing people first, and business second. I spent time getting to know the amazing humans on the other end of the call, and heard exclamations like, *"Jen, we HAVE to work with you."* Even the leads and gigs I ended up turning down said similar things, like, *"when I get to the level where I can afford you…I'll be calling back."*

It wasn't just gigs that were suddenly streaming in, there were also some huge new clients. One in particular was responsible for massively changing the trajectory and growth of our business that first year learning from Dani Johnson.

One year prior, I had been invited to the Billboard Music Awards—NOT because I had any reason to actually be invited, but as the guest of an honorable older gentleman who had been a producer on a film I worked on. I had seen billboards that the show was in town, and I got a hold of him, simply hoping to see my friend while he happened to be in town, and he ended up inviting me to the show. I sat next to two others he had given tickets to. Now, here we were, a year later, and one of those two was reaching out because the new company he was working for was in need of graphics help—a lot of it!

As we went through negotiations, I was able to use the new skills and tools that I had learned at the conference. When the contract was finalized, the new stream brought in so much work in one month that I had to hire, not one, but two additional contractors to help with the load. Our team was multiplying before my very eyes (and I didn't even like math!! I do now. I like it a lot! Especially when it makes more of itself).

It's important to note here that the business growth in that moment isn't the big thing. Prior to going to this conference, I only ever viewed myself as an artist. I never thought of myself as a businesswoman! I had no idea what it takes to run a business. How could I even think of starting a business when people think they're hiring me? I'm not duplicatable; my art is not duplicatable!

(Wow. I just now got a revelation of the limiting belief I had put on myself, my dreams, and my future. Thankfully that all changed. And it changed fast.)

Again if I could go back to this day, I'd say:

"Yes, Jen!!! It is time for that label to come off! You know the Voice that created you, who leads

you, and who has done the imaginable in your life up until now! Why would you doubt Him in any area? He can do all things!

"Remain teachable. You have found a coach who has a genuine heart to show you the way. Stay humble. Learn all that you can. I've seen what the Voice continues to do as He shows you every step of the way. Trust Him. Trust what He has led you to. It is so good. He is so good! He is doing a new thing!"

I can't tell you how many people I told about my breakthrough at the conference. I urged them all to go; to invest in themselves. The responses are pretty consistent. The most common excuse I get is, *"but I can't afford to attend something like that!"* I couldn't either. At my first event, I was so broke that I literally had zero dollars coming in that month. When my new South African friend, Linda was in line in front of me at a coffee shop, and offered to buy my coffee, I wanted to cry. The numbers were clear: I couldn't afford not to go. Quite frankly, leaving that first conference, there was something inside me that continued to shout, *"I want tacos!!!"*...wait no, wrong voice, I mean the Voice that kept shouting *"You HAVE to go back."*

At that point, I didn't care what it took; I knew that shout inside me was right. Whatever it was going to take, I had to go to the next conference. Despite the gigs that were coming in, I was broke. It wasn't a quick fix. I didn't suddenly have boatloads of money that I didn't know what to do with. I had debt!! I had crazy debt. I had bills. And I had a life I didn't know how to pay for. Not to mention all that I would have to pay for if I wanted to go back. But I knew that no matter what it was going to cost me, I had to get back there.

I was realistic: I knew it was going to get harder before it got better, especially if I was going to take it all seriously and continue to go back. I knew that I would have to be willing to take a huge risk and a huge leap of faith to invest into my future, if I was going to see it pay off.

My heart was telling me one thing, but my checkbook was telling me something different. I knew I couldn't trust my own instincts, like the time I got lost in Detroit with a map of Dublin. That was a long day. It was more of a gamble to listen only to myself. I trusted this coach and the people all around me at the conference. And we know the odds of gambling: the house wins and you don't. When I looked at the results of those who had committed to continuing to go back to conferences, working on themselves, I knew the right thing to do. Every single one of them had come out on top—and not just by a little.

I took the leap and went back to that very next conference a month later. I had to put everything on a credit card: my room, my flight, my food, everything! But the first morning of this event, there was that Voice again, shouting loudly through a random text from Braidon, a friend from the film industry, who had ZERO idea where I was, or that I was attending my second conference with this woman who had so profoundly impacted me. The text read: *"Morning friend! You just popped into my heart this morning. Wanted to say how thankful I am for you. You are such an inspiration. It's hard to lead and be a leader, but God has placed you here for a reason. He loves you so very much."*

I was flabbergasted. Here I was, at a conference, taking a huge financial risk, plus the risk of looking like I was going crazy, and this message arrives. It hit me with such power and authority that I knew the simultaneous peace and chills that came over me were confirmation that I was supposed to be here.

I came in this time with high expectations, while also wondering if it could really be THAT life-altering and impactful a second time. Sure enough, it didn't take long for that question to be answered. Everything seemed to soar to new levels. During the first break, as I was filling in my notes, all of a sudden, I heard someone speaking to me...it was Dani herself! She had picked me out in the crowd of 700 people. She delivered a quick message and shook my hand, exclaiming, *"I'm glad to see you back again."* Too shocked by the moment to say what my heart wanted to say, I just smiled. Had the words actually come out, I would have blabbered something like, "*I can't imagine a better place to be than right here.*" It was true. It may have only been the first session, but I knew I had made the right decision. I knew that the Voice was up to something more powerful than even I could comprehend.

I left that conference knowing I HAD to keep coming back. I know it sounds crazy. It sounded crazy to my mom who, for the first time, started to question the decisions I was making. No joke, my mom had NEVER questioned the decisions I had made in anything in my life, and now she decides to start. But I completely understood. I looked crazy!! Remember friend, I had ZERO dollars coming in when I went to my first conference; I had to borrow the money to get there, and I was just starting to see things turn around. Going into the second one, I had to put it ALL on a credit card. And you want to go to a THIRD one, Jen?! You're nuts!! But as nuts as I looked, and as strongly as I felt the burn to continue to go back...there was that Voice again, in the midst of everything brewing around me and within me.

As soon as I got home, I called Braidon, the film friend who texted me. As I was sharing how perfectly-timed his message was, he stopped me and said, *"there's more...your voice...your voice is going to be important. You also have the authority to MOVE what you think can't be moved."*

This friend had NO idea what I was wrestling with, and how conflicted I felt with my own desire to be radical. But as he spoke, I heard that Voice confirming what was brewing inside me.

A few days later, I was at a concert, watching the lyrics pop up onto the screen. All of a sudden, in bright bold letters, were the words, *"I'm going ALL-IN. Head first into the deep end. I hear you calling. And this time the fear won't win. I'm going, I'm going all in."* HAH!!! Here's your sign! There was that Voice, talking back to the voices of doubt that tried to creep in—loudly! It made an interesting parallel, as the theme of that second conference was: *"Stop feeding your fear. Build faith! It'll lead you to your future!"*

Before I went back for my THIRD event, more results sprouted up. I saw a whole art department unify in a beautiful way, thanks to using the skills Dani taught me. Several crew members came up to me privately and shared how much they appreciated the way I talked to people and genuinely cared. It was true, I did really care—I always had. But I had a whole new basket of skillsets and tools at my disposal, thanks to my coach, and it was taking my life—and the lives of people around me—to a whole new level.

I was so serious about having epic change that I was listening to recordings from the event every single day, even as I put in 12-hour days working a feature film. Driving to and from the gig every day, I'd play the audios in my car. There was no room for excuses! My future was too important; people were too important! Thanks to listening to those audios every day on that one film, I saw immediate results in my relationships.

As I drove to the wrap party (nervous as ever), Dani's voice was in my head, telling me exactly what to do. I did exactly what she said, and apparently it worked, because one crew member that night introduced me to his friend this way: *"Have you met my wife, Jen?!"* The other crew replied back, *"Um, excuse me but that's MY wife."* I was neither of their wives. And I had only had a couple interactions with each of them during production. That just shows how powerful interpersonal skills are. I was intentional with the words I spoke at that wrap party. In those moments, the words I chose lit them both up completely!

That's the influence of a powerful coach.

And it wasn't just the crew. My boss shared later that HIS boss had said, *"I really like that Jen. She's seriously amazing, and she has the BEST attitude. We have to continue working with her."*

Friend, I don't say this to toot my own horn; they're just evidence, that what this coach had been teaching me was changing my life POWERFULLY, and fast.

CHAPTER 14

"You Can Do This"

Faithful With The Little,
Setting The Foundation

Life was happening so fast, and the results were so
outstanding that, here I was at just my third event, and I
knew I was going ALL-IN—not just with words, but with
action. I walked to the back of the room that first day
with a pep in my step as I executed my plan to purchase
literally EVERY teaching product Dani was selling. Still
broke, mind you, but completely LEAPING into it all with
my actions. One of my new friends, Diane, who continued
to speak LIFE into my journey those next few years, came
over and prayed over me right then and there. The minute
I opened my eyes, there was another leader from the
company waiting to speak to me. He asked, *"would you*

be willing to share your story on stage in 5 minutes?"

What?!!? You want me to speak? I'm new to all this!! Weird as it seemed, I also knew that, here I was, once again being offered a microphone to speak what THE Voice was doing. With no clue what I was going to share, I said yes.

I took the next few minutes and used what I learned back in college to start speaking life into my own mind and spirit. I visualized it going well.

As the next session started, they called me on stage to share what had happened since those first two events. I was so moved that the Voice had led me to yet another dream coming true: simply getting to tell the world how good that Voice was and how much that Voice loves them. I shared that my story wasn't over, and neither was theirs!

But that wasn't the only thing I shared. When they asked on stage, *"If you could pick one thing, that impacted you the most, what would it be?"* I knew my answer, It was easy. I replied, *"Oh yea, it was the principle of **'He who is faithful with the little will be trusted with much.'"** That one takeaway started to turn everything around for me.

I was amazing at handling money when it came to my job. When I was given a project and a budget, I knew

where every single penny was going. I felt it was my duty
to the job and those who had hired me and entrusted
me with it, to know where it was all going. It was a real
responsibility. After all, how many creatives know how to
handle a budget right?!

But while I was amazing at handling other people's
money, I was horrible at handling my own. I had no idea
where MY money was going every month. Don't get me
wrong, I was paying my bills (mostly) on time, but I had
no idea every month if I would have enough. Most of the
time, I didn't. I knew coming home from that first event
that I was going to HAVE to change that part of my life if
I wanted to come back to future conferences—and you've
heard how badly I wanted to come back. I even thought
that I couldn't figure out a budget because, as a freelancer,
I never knew what I was going to be making each month.
But that was just an excuse that kept me from figuring out
a way to take action. Once I sat down and started to figure
it all out, and established a plan to start tracking where
every penny was going, it all started to change.

I didn't just track it, I made a PLAN for where the
money was going to go before I even had it. There was no
way my money was ever going to go anywhere other than
where I told it to go. That principle changed everything.

I could feel the tears coming in as I got to introduce

this coach who had so profoundly impacted me. I cried watching a video clip of just a glimpse of the lives she had changed. I couldn't believe I had the honor to simply shout her name as she walked onto the stage. I was all-in.

+++++

Later that day, I got a tap on my shoulder and a new friend whispered in my ear, *"Check your messages."* There was a message letting me know that my new coach wanted to interview me on her television show. I was stunned, and felt the tears come up again. I couldn't believe all that was playing out in front of me. And I absolutely took it deadly serious. Returning home, I prepared for that interview.

One day, I accidentally left my notes out on the kitchen counter in my apartment. My roommate, Elissa saw them when I wasn't home, read them, and shared with me later how it impacted her. I knew this Voice was up to even more. At this time, she really wasn't sure what she thought of this Voice, but I continued to pour into her.

She shared that, when she read the notes for my interview, she was so inspired: *"I know you know I don't get excited about much,"* she confessed, *"but it made me excited to go to the conference with you! You are so talented and amazing and you're going to kill it! And more importantly, touch so many lives. I love you!"* She had been watching what had been happening to me since attending that first event, but hadn't decided to come herself yet. At last I saw a glimpse of the friend I had been praying for for the last two years. This Voice start leading her, drawing her in to what would change her life over the next year too.

The interview was awesome: I got to interact with this coach that was changing my life, but I also got to share what that Voice had done in my life with all those listening. The interview was published and shared all over social media with this headline:

> *"We all go through tough times. It's unavoidable! However, your reaction to those seasons determines whether you ultimately triumph-or fail. And, today we have the ultimate inspiration and encouragement for when you do encounter those times. So join Dani today for this uplifting episode of the Dani Johnson show, as she interviews Jen Horling, a woman who continued to persevere in the face of terrible tragedy and refused to settle for less than she knew God had in store for her. Trust me...this episode is for you!"*

I could have died happy in that moment. The last 14 years of my life could not have been summarized or put to purpose more poetically. What The Voice had done was being told to the world. The pain it had walked me through—up to and BEYOND that interview—was being used to help someone else walking through their own story of tragedy.

+++++

That Voice continued to work beyond the conference and the interview, as new project leads came in for more art department work. One of them skyrocketed our hope for the following year, asking us to think about what our small graphics team would need to do to be ready to be doing over six figures' worth of work for just them.

But while all the awesome external results were happening, and I was starting to see that part of life start to turn around, that wasn't the most exciting part to me. I was moved by what the Voice was doing within me and to the friends and family around me. Those stories are the ones that are the most worth telling. As I prepared myself for the next event—a leadership development conference called *Creating A Dynasty*—little did I know what would happen within me (and around me) at that event.

What that first *Creating A Dynasty* event did within me was way more powerful than anything that had happened at any of the three *First Steps To Success* events. At *Creating A Dynasty*, we dug deep into several roots that had been hiding in my soul.

Remember back in Chapter 1, when I said that I had let several labels and limiting beliefs take over in my thinking? Well, at *Creating A Dynasty* we started to address all that.

There was one label that had taken quite a stand in my heart and mind prior to attending any events: I had gotten to a place where I had ZERO interest in getting married. In fact, to be honest, it had become a NEGATIVE desire—I was actively avoiding relationships. My desire had a negative in front of it. Maybe even a few gremlins standing guard that, anytime anyone even ever thought about it with me, they'd glare their slimy green teeth, drool a bit, and blow kisses. Who doesn't want to kiss that?! Interests were bouncing right off of me (and them).

I felt like the vision that had been laid on my heart was too important to turn my attention to marriage. I felt a burning obligation that I had to help people, and it made no sense to let my heart get attached to anything else. Not to mention the fact that I didn't see anyone anywhere that looked overwhelmingly happy to be married. It looked hard—even miserable! So I absolutely believe I lost any inkling of an interest that I might have ever had.

But as I went through *Creating A Dynasty*, something powerful happened. Dani's husband, Hans spoke during one of the sessions, and then she joined him on stage. She shared how much MORE they've been able to do for others together—and something happened inside of me.

I watched this woman, whose heart for others had so profoundly impacted me, work in tandem with her husband to help people. It was like a small shift physically manifested within me, and my spirit exclaimed, *"I want that!"*

My response shocked me. This didn't fit what I believed about myself. But as I shared this with a friend, she said something that beautifully clarified what had just happened: *"Jen, for the first time, you saw marriage as more than just about you. It became about other people. And for the first time, it became attractive to you."* She was right, but that doesn't mean I was ready! HAH! Those gremlins were still wreaking havoc.

But then, Dani announced that she would be holding a marriage conference. My mind raced: I knew what she would say to me if she could hear my thoughts, so I did exactly what I heard her say in my head, *"Kiss a gremlin!!!"* Ah! No, that's not what I heard. It was *"Run TOWARD your fear!!!"* So I did exactly that.

I ran to the back of the room and got in line to sign up for a conference completely about marriage. Bahahahaha!!! (I hope you're laughing with me, because I was definitely laughing at myself as I stood waiting in that line, in disbelief at what I was doing.)

I heard other voices in my head as I stood in line: *"Jen, what the heck are you doing? You don't want to get married!!"* I told them to SHUT UP; I knew that, whatever had just happened in my heart, I wanted to give the Voice room to do more if He wanted to. I had a hunch he wanted to lock up those gremlins and send them into a pit.

With everything that had happened at this conference, I felt like that Voice was back to His old tricks, leaning down toward me and subtly and softly tapping on my heart, just like He had at my first conference with Dani. I felt loved and seen. It was just like the time I was working on a film and after a fun night of hanging out a bonfire with the crew, I went back to my room early. I figured no one would even notice. But then I heard a knock on my door, there stood the director, Dennis. He looked me in the eyes and said, *"NO,"* and then picked me up and threw me over his shoulder to take me back out to the party. I felt seen. Valued. He wasn't going to let me be left behind.

After *Creating A Dynasty*, crazy things started happening before I even got home. That Voice was ready to move mountains! Waiting at the airport, a random woman noticed my t-shirt from the event and Googled "Creating A Dynasty" and "Dani Johnson," to see what they were. She walked over to me and started asking me questions about it! I was so shocked by the boldness of this woman. We talked for over an hour as she shared about her life and how this sounded like something she needed. I encouraged her to come and followed up with her later, and that was great. But I was so blown away by what the Voice was doing, and who He was connecting me to, just through the words on my t-shirt! That bright orange t-shirt became a kind of beacon as it drew a couple from the Netherlands who had been at the event. We swapped stories and our takeaways from our powerful weekend.

As I boarded my flight, I had the feeling that the Voice had certain people for me to "run into." It was Dean Cain again—oh my gosh!!! (No I'm kidding, it wasn't him.) It was a woman from Australia and her sister, who had also been at the event. As she saw me, she called out, *"Hey!!! It's Jen!! Haha."* I didn't recognize her, but she had seen a video from the conference where I was shared my story on stage, and recognized me—all the way from her home in Australia! I was delighted to know there was a purpose in such an appointment. There was no other way to explain how SHE ended up sitting next to me. We spent the rest of the flight swapping life stories and reflecting on the event. As the flight went on and we spoke over the dreams and visions on both of our hearts, that Voice poured life into both of us.

That Voice was on a ROLL!

Shortly after returning home, I made plans to travel

out to Los Angeles for a film conference with Shane, a great friend from the film industry. It was our second year in a row taking this trip together. Shane was a friend who also listened to—and valued the presence of—that Voice in his life. Going into the trip, we were intentional about never being too concrete in any of our plans, but rather positioning ourselves to be open to whatever that Voice might want to do, or who He might want to pour life into that we might meet. We were listening for it.

On the four hour drive to Los Angeles from Nevada, I felt the nudge to call a friend on the other side of the country. He didn't answer, but he texted right away saying he wasn't doing so well at the moment. I called him right back, but when he answered there was no greeting, just the sound of sobbing. I immediately started speaking love over him, telling him how much he was loved and valued, He cried even harder.

After a few minutes, he gained his composure and shared his story: this amazing and insanely-talented friend had tried to kill himself earlier that year on Easter and was thinking about it again. Through my tears, I continued to tell him how much he was loved. *"Jen"* He said, *"Everyone has been so concerned that I wasn't getting out of the house right now or whether or not I was eating, but all I wanted to hear was that somebody loved me! I can't believe that that was the first words that came out of your mouth!"*

Every time I look back on this story, there's no doubt in my mind that it wasn't just me when I answered his call. What came out of me was from more than just me. It was that Voice, letting my friend know who he was and how loved he was. That was an appointment. Had that Voice not nudged me, I don't know to this day what would have happened to my friend. I'm so grateful for it's presence and it's power that day. There's no doubt in my life it saved my friend's life.

Shane, who had been driving with me the whole time, had been so inspired by our conversations and learning how I commit to things, I shared with him how those moments come with a lot of fear, but I choose to enter into them anyway. He encouraged me to shoot a video share it more publicly. I obliged and shared much of what you have read in this book, but especially my fear of public speaking.

After I shared that video, I was shocked by how many people responded privately. Responding to each one, I heard so many crazy stories of what others were going through, but was also so encouraged by how my video had inspired them. That Voice was working in people's lives through me, in spite of me.

One in particular, Jenny, was a complete stranger to

me at that time. She had lost her fire-fighting husband just three months prior. We had never met, but I was able to encourage her in the moment from my own experience of loss. I knew how she felt—and how her children felt. I knew how to pour life into her in that darkness.

+++++

I wish I could say I was a total ROCK and could handle all the intensity that was coming my way, but so much happened in just one week that I started to get overwhelmed.

It climaxed when I another close friend on the other side of the country—one whom I REALLY cared for— abruptly texted me, letting me know she, too, was suicidal. I frantically tried to call her, but couldn't get a hold of her, no matter what I did. At the same time, I got word that my uncle had a heart attack and was going into open heart surgery. I had also recently learned, that his wife (my aunt) had been diagnosed with Stage IV cancer. I grew up across the street from them; they were like second parents to me. Fortunately, another local close friend, Jax called and we chatted for over an hour as I broke down. She poured so much life into me.

In that call I had one of the biggest realizations of my life: I wasn't just hitting a crisis point because I was overwhelmed, life was boiling over because my spirit was.

On my arm is a tattoo that says, *"I will never leave you or forsake you."* I had gotten it years ago because I needed that reminder every single day, after I lost my dad. Those words spoke life into me every day and kept me going. But that phone call was the first time the "or forsake you" part really came to life for me.

As I was explaining my journey and why I was feeling overwhelmed, I realized that I had another secret that I hadn't been willing to share with anyone. I hadn't really been honest with myself about it. I was afraid that if anyone knew what I am about to share with you that people I cared about would walk away. It was in this conversation that I voiced for the first time, *"I can't worry about those who might leave me, because that story is not for them…it's for those who are hurting and feel like they have no one to talk to. If Dani can be as bold as she is with her story, and the ugly side of her story…I can too! Look at how many people she's helping because she's so transparent with her pain!"*

CHAPTER 15

"You Are So Loved"

The Breakthrough

I did not see this coming.

That Voice was working so strongly that I felt compelled to send a video relaying the breakthrough to the people who run Dani's conferences. There was a part of my story that I wasn't exactly ready to share publicly, but I had felt a nudge that maybe someday I would.

The video started out innocently enough: I shared with them how excited I was knowing that I now had a place where I could send the hurting people that kept showing up in my life. I talked about Jenny (the woman who had just lost her firefighter husband), how she came to her first event and found a community and the wisdom to improve her life in every area-her finances, her debt, her kids…you name it. I saw the desperate cry on my heart be answered in wanting to help people MORE than with just a prayer. I shared stories of people's lives I had seen transform.

But that's when I shared a very personal piece of my story that I never thought I would share. I never quite felt ready for it to get out, but here I had said it.

I shared that, if this Voice could do all that He had done with my story of loss, plus Jenny's story, PLUS everything He was doing for Elissa (who had just come to her first event, too), then He could do something amazing with the other story too. I felt like I was finally stepping off the super-high diving board, but I knew it was time.

Now I want to share it with you.

At that last conference, Dani had shared how she had struggled with intimidation. I have no idea if she saw me as she shared, but I lost it. Tears were streaming down my face. I realized this was why I had felt trapped for all these years; why I felt like I couldn't talk to anyone about something I really struggled with. I felt trapped because I worried about whether people were still going to love me, or if they would leave me.

Ever since my first *First Steps To Success* conference,

I knew that Voice had been working on me and gently tapping on a specific area of my heart—an area I felt I couldn't talk to anyone about in full transparency.

In the video I referenced the two close friends who told me they were suicidal, and how I had been overwhelmed by the depth of emotion I felt for both of them. But with the second friend, I couldn't get a hold of her for days. For days, I didn't know if my friend was dead or alive. This one hit me even harder than the first. As I watched these two friends suffer, I knew that I couldn't worry anymore about who might leave me if they knew my dark truth. Because it wasn't for them. I needed to share my story for those who were hurting in silence and felt like they had no one to talk to. I cared more about the ones who felt that way, because it had been me.

I had grown up in church and in Christian circles. I never felt safe to talk to anyone about my struggle without them losing all respect for me. But more than the fear of the loss of respect, I feared losing everyone who had walked with me through the loss of my dad. That fear trapped me. I was afraid that I would lose more people if I was honest about things I was going through.

So what was the big secret?

I had developed feelings for a woman in another city. I didn't want to admit it to myself—and definitely not to her—but it was true, and when that relationship ended, I felt completely alone in going through that loss. When it ended, I suffered. Unless you could see into the deepest part of my heart, my grieving might have seemed extreme. Even my mom—the closest person to me in the world—couldn't understand why I was struggling with it the way I was, and why I felt like I couldn't talk to anybody about it. But I was sure I couldn't talk to anybody but that Voice.

I don't think it is intentional, by any means, but I hate the intimidation that the church has created where we feel like we can't talk to each other about certain things, like what we're feeling. Sometimes we don't know whether our feelings are right or wrong. But it wouldn't have even mattered to me at that point, whether it was right or wrong, because I had experienced it. Right or wrong, I had felt something, and it was real. I needed to make sense of those feelings. But I couldn't talk about them. I needed to know WHY.

Please hear me out; I'm NOT saying I hate the church. I love the church!! I grew up in the church, and it helped save my life (and so much more). What I'm talking about is the dang GIANT pink elephant in the room—the one no one talks about. And when someone does talk about it, it's usually to make their strong negative opinions known on the matter, not to simply listen to a hurting heart.

Can you imagine what would happen if, instead of sharing our opinion about something, we just listened to the heart on the other side? At that time, all I needed to hear was how much the Voice loved me as I dealt with those thoughts on that journey. I needed to know that I wasn't alone and I wouldn't be abandoned if I voiced it.

I didn't grow up having feelings for either gender, I had simply fallen in love with a friends' heart, and it just happened to be a woman. But again, I didn't voice any of that in that season—I didn't trust that I'd be safe! I didn't want to know what anyone thought of what I was feeling, because it wouldn't have changed the fact that I had experienced it, and those feelings were real. It was that realness that I needed to understand.

I knew what was finally coming out of me thanks to watching Dani process her own intimidation. The Voice had been nudging me about these feelings, and He wanted me to let Him help.

But I still felt trapped. I was trapped by the lie that, if I voiced my struggle, I would LOSE everyone. What a lie that was! Had I not broken free this year, who knows the depths that trapped heart might have sunk to? If anyone ever asked me how I viewed my future in this area, they often heard me say, *"All I know is that I believe that Voice can do the same with my heart as he has done with my career."* And while that belief was true, I still felt stuck. I never felt safe to share the depth of that feeling with anyone, but I knew that Voice would have quite the challenge if I were to ever get there.

All I could see was that I would stay trapped forever, completely alone. I saw two roads:

1) I could marry a man, but if I did I'd always wonder, *"what about those other feelings?"* That wouldn't be fair to whoever I married, because my heart would be confused. I didn't want to hurt anyone!

2) I could enter a relationship with a woman. But if I did that, I'd always wonder, *"what the One I love the most—that Voice—would think of me? I couldn't risk hurting the one I love the most."*

So I felt completely trapped by my own fear.

Listening to Dani and the "nakedness" with which she shared her story, I knew I needed to be "naked" with my full story if I were going to reach the hurting. Watching my suicidal friends, I knew I cared more for helping others like them who were hurting.

I didn't have answers for whether my feelings were right or wrong; I can only tell you my experience. I hope you hear how much that Voice loves you, no matter what you may be struggling with. You can't shock Him. I know He's the only one I desired to hear from! He was the only one that KNEW how I was feeling and what I had experienced.

It's important to mention here something else that happened.

In sharing my struggle with Dani's team, one woman's response was pivotal. Diane is an amazingly wise woman that I admire so much. Not only did she celebrate the release that happened inside my spirit in voicing it with them, but I vividly remember what she said to my questions later, as I continued through this journey and tried to understand what I had experienced: *"Jen, it's not about whether it's right or wrong...you had an experience, and that experience was real. There's no doubt in my mind you loved her; those feelings were real. What matters is that maybe that Voice is trying to give you something even better."* Her acceptance of where I was at emotionally and the confusion I was in allowed me to feel safe, and gave me room to grow.

Finally, I opened up to another film friend about all that my heart had been through, knowing he had been through a similar journey. He said, *"Jen, six months ago the Voice put it on my heart that you were struggling in this area,"* and then shared how he had been praying for me for six months about THIS!! He also shared that just as I started to open up to him, he simultaneously heard fireworks go off down the street. *"He is so happy you are finally releasing that!!"* That's exactly what the breakthrough was: a release. I was set free!

That freedom didn't stop there. That Voice continued to lead and speak powerfully in this area. Just wait until you hear the rest of what He said and did with this part of the journey. That's precisely what I wish I could have told myself years ago, going through it.

Again, if I could go back to this day, I'd say:

"Yes Jen!!! This is so huge for you! He is proud of you! You are breaking free from so many limiting beliefs and lies!

"I know how hard this was for you. Take heart. He loves you, sees you and believes in you. He has overcome the world! I know the things this Voice is saying to you and leading you to! They are worth it! He is worth it! Keep trusting in that Voice.

"More and more freedom will come—more than you could ever imagine! Just take it one step at a time. Take his hand. Listen for his Voice. He is a good father. He will not rush you any faster than your heart is ready to go. But you can trust him!

I've seen the journey He will take your on, and it is so good!

"I bless the journey yet ahead of you. I bless you with clarity. I bless you with life! I bless you with love!"

CHAPTER 16

"Where Is Your Faith?"

Breaking Free From Fear

Wow, okay. So now you know my dark secret, but we've only cracked that egg. That egg still needs to be cooked!

I confessed EVERYTHING to this woman I'd had feelings for years ago, and in the process, my heart got completely shattered. Fearing that I would lose her completely as a friend, I knew that it could snowball into being cut out of her life for a second time, and just as harshly as the first time.

I got on my knees and asked the Voice, *"if this ends the relationship with someone I love so deeply, I'm going to need you more than ever, especially this weekend."*

I was heading into another *First Steps to Success* event that weekend. As I watched that weekend go by, this time in Atlanta, I watched a cycle repeat in my life. It took me back 7 years, to that terrible breakup I had suffered. But this time, something different was swirling over me.

As I went through the steps of forgiving myself and others, I knew I was going to have to forgive this person. She had wounded me deeply during a vulnerable time of finally being honest with myself and being bold enough to release it.

I completely broke down as I walked through this process, but then something powerful happened. The entire weekend, Dani kept hammering the same phrase: ***"where is your faith?!"*** But as she said it, I suddenly saw a flash of a memory appear before me playing like a movie in front of my eyes—a moment from 14 years prior that I had completely forgotten about.

In the flash, I saw myself sitting with the Christian counselor I was seeing shortly after my dad had died. I heard him explaining why loss was always going to hit me so much harder than the normal person: *"people who go through tragedy and tragic loss experience grief in a much deeper and more sorrowful way. Their process is a* lot more intensified and painful, as well as prolonged." As I heard those words again in the flash, I saw myself on the couch, suddenly snap at Him with my finger pointed at Him:

"NO! WHERE IS YOUR FAITH?!"

Suddenly, more phrases hurtled through the air from the left side of the room in front of me: fears and lies that had trapped and crippled me.

"You can't lose her again, you can't go through that loss again! And this time, you know what those feelings were." From the right side of the room I saw another phrase come against it and smash it to smithereens, like a rock: **"NO! WHERE IS YOUR FAITH?!"**

Then there was another phrase flashing from the left: "You can't contact your family, you've already forgiven them! What if they abuse you again?!" The right side shouted back again, smashing it to smithereens: **"NO! WHERE IS YOUR FAITH?!"**

The left side voices called: "You can't tell your mom why you're hurting as much as you are right now. It will hurt her, and she's already been through too much! What if she doesn't understand?" The right side shouted back, smashing it to smithereens: **"NO! WHERE IS YOUR FAITH?!"**

The left side wasn't done yet: *"You can't do any of it Jen, It's too overwhelming."* The right side of my brain shouted back: ***"NO! WHERE IS YOUR FAITH?!"***... smithereens.

I saw myself SHOUT back to every single fear that flew in front of me, showing its horrible head of lies. It was as if a literal ROCK flew up opposite each lie and completely smashed it to oblivion. I blame my love of superheroes for this image. I was definitely Wonder Woman-ing that crap up. (Side note; you should definitely ask to see the Wonder Woman tattoo on the inside of my forearm if we ever meet).

Just like that, the world in my head was quiet and I watched the dust from all those smithereens drift in the breeze.

But I saw what the Voice had done through my life already (taking my career and love for people to heights I never imagined) and I shouted back, *"THAT'S THE VOICE!!!"*

Then I heard, ***"Jen, you'll be unstoppable now."***

But facing my biggest fears in my brain (all dressed up like Wonder Woman) is one thing. Leaving the event, I knew it was time to put the suit on and face them in the real world.

I went home with a fierce new determination to face my fears. But first, the Voice wanted to fill my tank to the top. We were in Atlanta and I was invited over to the house of a couple I had met at the conferences, who lived nearby. As we all shared our different experiences and breakthroughs from the weekend, one specific friend, Chris, shared, *"The Lord allows in His wisdom what He can prevent in His power"* (Ezekiel 47). He talked about how that Voice allows jagged rocks to be dropped into the middle of the river of His flow and His intimacy. He allows things to happen to us, so that, by the washing of the water (His word), these jagged rocks that once impeded the flow get washed over and become smooth river stones in time. He went on to share that David went and picked up five smooth river stones and used them to take down Goliath. He explained that Dani had given me a smooth river stone *("where is your faith")* and I used it as I confronted every single lie that had attacked me.

That weekend was really a spiritual battle for me. It was my eighth conference with Dani, and a friend pointed out to me that there was a Biblical meaning behind that number: eight is the number for new beginnings. Here I was, at my eighth event, fighting through it to gain a new beginning, and on the heels of using the smooth river stones to take down my own Goliath, I had received a bigger vision for my business. I could see the real calling the Voice had on my life, and how He was going to use it to tell stories about how people have overcome things. I could encourage people to overcome and persevere through their challenges, because I hadn't given in to suicide—I didn't let the jagged rocks cut me.

People in a fatherless world need something to identify with that's greater than themselves. This is why so many superhero movies were crushing it at the box office at the time—because they create a hope in people: they give people something bigger to believe in. Because of what I've overcome, and the skills he's given me, I am able to reach a larger audience and help them take down the Goliaths in their own lives.

Wow! Right?!

How's that for an epic ending of a weekend in the presence of that Voice? I bet you can guess what I did next! I went home and auditioned for Wonder Woman.... NOT. I went home and faced my fears.

CHAPTER 17

"You Can Trust Me, Even In The Things You Don't Understand"

A Reset On Love

That Voice was not done yet! Hot on the heels off that event in Atlanta, I thought, surely there was NO WAY a weekend could get any better (I've learned to stop saying that). Just wait until you read what this Voice said next!

Between the Atlanta event and the next event, I received four things:

1. I got a new understanding about loss and it's effects on my future. I believed there was nothing that Voice couldn't do, that NOTHING was too difficult

for Him, and my future was longer subject to
another BOMB of loss that might someday defeat
me.

2. I opened up fully to my mom about everything.
    While it didn't go perfectly, I finally felt free. It
    felt amazing that I could now be fully transparent
    about my journey with the person I loved the most,
    my mom.

3. I contacted the abusers in my family (but only after
    covering it with prayer, asking that Voice to put
    up a spiritual barrier of protection, so that nothing
    negative or hurtful or abusive could pass through).
    I applied what we had learned and just FORGAVE
    them and asked THEM for forgiveness. Crazily
    enough, they informed me they would be visiting
    my city that very weekend on the opposite side of
    the country. So we made arrangements to meet
    for lunch. It was the first time in five years where
    nothing of the past was brought up and no abuse
    happened. It just was life looking forward. It was so
    good!! I was amazed.

4. I let go of that friend. It hurt, and took time, but I
    chose to let that Voice continue leading, one day at a
    time, and chose to trust that He would be with me.

I did it all!

I didn't face those fears alone; that Voice was truly with me. One of the most beautiful glimpses of just how present He was came during a workout one evening.

Early on, exercise became the zone where I processed my feelings. In this season, I actually started pushing myself harder physically, just as I pushed myself mentally and spiritually. I knew that if I ever wanted to get to the level of physical fitness I wanted, I needed to take action, so I joined a CrossFit group. Several months in, having just faced and worked through some of my biggest fears, I was also going through tremendous heartbreak. My heart had been completely shattered. So, as I continued to push myself further and further in that workout, and I neared reaching my physical limit, feeling like my whole body was about to burst and collapse to the ground, my mind was racing. I was processing through every emotion I was feeling and the heartbreak I was carrying. I felt like no one knew how I really felt; no one understood the weight of the hurt I was going through.

As I pushed myself every additional second, I felt the weight of those words growing, I felt the tears rise. But just as I was about to burst into tears, I heard a subtle Voice whisper, *"I understand."* That Voice had heard the entire dialogue in my head, even though I hadn't said a word. He had heard it and He cared! Those two words meant everything to me. No one else could understand everything I had been through, but that Voice could.

Going into that leadership conference, I had already faced my biggest fears. That Voice was so intimate with me all weekend, speaking into the very cracks and crevices where it was needed. And while there had been so many powerful moments across a year of these conferences, this one moment seemed to most poetically summarize that year. I could name countless amazing external results:

- How by the end of that first year I had paid off over $10,000 in debt, WHILE also going to every single event all across the country.

- How my graphic design business had tripled its numbers from the previous year.

- How it went from having just one design contractor to a team of over seven and growing.

- How one-year prior, I had ZERO dollars coming in that month.

I could tell you about gig after gig I had received in just that first year—gigs I had never dreamed of getting to work on. But as amazing as the external results were, it was the internal work that was even more powerful to me. It was what had been happening to my heart that entire first year: the daddy/daughter *"you can trust me"* message that He had spoken to me so intimately.

Beyond being just broke and frustrated, I was also deeply broken, and I didn't even know it. I hadn't admitted it to even myself until that weekend. As I reflected over that first year with my coach, and the anniversary that was coming up, something massive hit me.

I realized that the VERY night before I left to attend my first event something could have happened. I was 35, and had been a virgin my whole life—by choice. And the reason behind that choice probably isn't something you're expecting to read next. It honestly wasn't for any religious purposes (as much as I'd like to believe that's what it was); it was a choice, and I was very serious about it, because I KNEW that if I went there with anyone, I'd be dead.

I get it: that sounds crazy. That's precisely why I didn't share that with anyone. I didn't think people would understand, so I wasn't overly vocal about it. I just knew that, if I got that close to someone, and they didn't stay in my life, my heart literally wouldn't be able to handle it. After everything I felt after losing my dad at 21, I knew that it would be a death sentence for me. I knew my heart couldn't handle intimate loss.

But at 35, after being a virgin my whole life, the night before I came to my first *First Steps To Success*, I could have very well barreled head first toward that "death." I made out with the young woman I had long had feelings for—the one who had broken my heart once before. Had circumstances not torn us apart (I had to leave at 4:00 a.m. that next morning to catch a flight), I know I would have, if the opportunity had been there.

Looking back on that night, and the year that followed, I could say with complete belief that the Voice had intervened. My coach was the vessel for HIS rescue! Had it not been for that event and that community, I would have headed straight down a track to my death that year. Instead, my Rescuer intervened and kept me on a track toward life! That Voice was fighting FOR me. He could see my heart and knew that it was on the brink of giving up on it all.

+++++

During the first evening of the second leadership conference, as all of that was hitting me, I got more opportunities to release some more of my old life, and I embraced every opportunity that was presented. While I don't remember exactly what Dani prayed when she laid her hand on my heart (I literally couldn't even hear her words, even though she was standing right in front of me), later that night, while I was in the shower, I experienced one of the most powerful moments of my life.

I had a daydream that I now believe was a vision from that Voice. In the daydream, God was standing next to me, and He looked over at me and said, *"All I needed you to do, Jen, was give me everything."* Then He extended His hand to me and said, *"Then take my hand, even with the things you don't understand. You can trust me. I'm your dad...and I'm a good dad."*

That whole weekend felt like a *"daddy/daughter you can trust me"* message, playing over and over again.

During that conference we were challenged to write out our views on different categories of our lives, and what we were going to CHOOSE to believe about them. As I did, I had a huge revelation. Starting at the top of my page, writing what I chose to believe, next to "myself," I wrote "limitless with God," which was a belief that matched my before belief. I saw myself as fearless and bold, because I knew I was limitless with that Voice. But as I went down the page with each category, it hit me, there was an area where I had been "limiting" myself and that Voice, an area where I thought I already knew the conclusion. It was almost as if that Voice was giving me a literal road map that tunneled my vision into exactly what He wanted me to see right then. Suddenly, I realized that I needed to take a step back and choose to stop limiting myself (and the Voice) in the area of relationships/marriage. I knew I needed to view that as an area of my life that should be "limitless with that voice," and I hadn't.

That Voice continued to lead my vision that weekend—gently, like a good dad—not rushing me, but simply showing me glimpses of how He wanted to lead. The first glimpse came through a funny interaction with a new friend and another through the "happenstance" of a moment, and powerfully through the words of another.

We were doing exercises in groups of four and Dani directed us to take a moment to ask the Voice what the others in our foursome needed to hear from Him, and say that. As those in my group spoke what they heard, I started to cry…hard. The tears started as the first person said to me, *"you are a GOOD friend,"* not knowing I was going through the loss of a deep friendship. The second person said, *"He wants you to share your story—your full story. We know there's more to you. And not only do we here crave to hear it from you, but the world needs it."*

What's even crazier is that, the three people who were in my group for this exercise all said the same thing to me, and none of them knew me prior to sitting together through that group. They knew nothing of all my internal battles. That Voice was powerfully making His presence known, powerfully confirming what He wanted to lead me to!

+++++

That wasn't the only rescue that happened. That

Voice continued to be busy, both in me and around me! As we neared the holidays, I "randomly" received a message from a woman who had been attending the same conferences, but was living all the way in Australia! She had just seen a social media post I had made about my dad, and mentioned that she was battling thoughts of suicide. I was so honored that she reached out to me. I talked with her for a long time, hearing where her heart was and speaking into the brokenness and darkness the best I knew how. I continued to follow up, and connected her with others in our community. Over the next few months I saw this woman's life LIGHT up! That Voice was now radiating RESCUE!

Before that year was over, I got hired to work on a Bollywood film. While it was an amazing and FUN opportunity, I questioned why I had even been needed, as the art wasn't very complex.

I learned rather quickly why that Voice had led me there. With what my heart was wrestling with, I wanted to HEAR from that Voice; to know what He thought! I wanted to know what the one I loved the most—the Voice—had to say. He saw my heart and what it felt. He knew what it had been through.

On that production, I truly believe He gave me that gift; but what's even crazier is how He delivered it. The first day of the production, I was making friends with the crew, who had come from all over to shoot in Las Vegas. Almost immediately, I hit it off with an older gentleman, Alejandro, with a thick accent from Brooklyn. Our friendship developed fast, and it wasn't long before he was sharing in great detail about a gay friend of his back in New York, and the struggles he was going through. What was strange about this sharing was that I had never once uttered my struggle to him. He couldn't have known who I had been attracted to. Yet over the entire two weeks of production, every day, he delivered more of this story to me. He even shared how he had been involved with a study for the government about same-sex attraction—whether people are born with it or it's something they choose—and the results they had found!!

WHAAAAAT?!? Have I mentioned yet that this man was very vocal about his love for (and trust in) that Voice?! So this man was sharing ALL of this with me, the friend's journey, the government study, and the Voice's presence amidst it all. And here I was, still saying NOTHING about my own journey. There's no doubt in my mind that this meeting had been a setup. That Voice knew I wanted to hear from HIM! And He knew how my heart had been wrestling and was finally being set free. And in that freedom, He met me with answers and guidance.

CHAPTER 18

"I Am Doing A NEW Thing"

An Epic Anniversary

As that first year came to come to a close, Dani invited anyone who was interested to take a trip with her to Israel. When the email for the details of the trip came through, a family member was visiting. As I read that the deposit would be due in two weeks, she asked, *"How are you going to pay for that?!"*

I responded, *"I don't know!! All I know is, if you look at what that Voice did this whole last year, why would I do anything else other than say FULL STEAM AHEAD to any fear or obstacle?!"* I threw my fist in the air and grinned. (Would you believe I also totally pictured myself as a choo-choo train as I said that? And I definitely think this family member thought I had literally blown a gasket).

That very next day, I got a call for an Art Director gig for a nationwide commercial. When they asked for my day rate, I said a number that I knew was high (although it wasn't unusual for high-end commercial work). I'll admit I clenched up a little, bracing for the answer, but she laughed, *"Oh girl...we can give you way more money than that!"* I think I laughed out loud in the call. I mean, is that the kind of response you usually get?! Well, they bumped it up another $150 bucks from what I asked for—and I thought I'd be making AMAZING money for 6 days—way more than I had even asked for. I was ecstatic, because I knew... there was my deposit for Israel!

Then the gig started and then we found out that the rate they told me wasn't going to work. Instead, they were going to be paying me much more! With that news, that single 6-day gig would pay for almost my entire trip!

I can't tell you how many times in that week I had tears in my eyes as I watched that Voice work. Each time, I flashed back to the daydream He gave me that night in my hotel room at that leadership conference.

Imagine my shock when I saw a video about the Israel trip, and heard Dani say, *"this is about a daddy/ daughter, father/son experience."* It was like that Voice was continuing to call me through her words, extending His hand back to me, leading me to things He wanted to show me. The Voice was providing the very funds I needed without question, days after saying, *"FULL STEAM AHEAD!"* If this was a train, I knew He wanted me to get on.

Before that train left the tracks, it had one more GIANT stop to make: another conference, held the weekend of January 12th, 2019. Little did I know how powerful and timely that stop would be.

Not only was it another life-changing weekend, but it had a unique significance. Not only was that weekend my official one-year anniversary since I had attended my first conference and completely committed to the entire year of training (nine conferences in total) and all the transformation that came with it, but it was also another anniversary.

The first evening of the conference, I gave a "thank you" card with a testimonial inside it to Dani and her team, thanking them for all that they had done for me that year. One of the leaders asked if I would be willing to share my story on stage the next morning. While shocked at the request, I knew the Voice was up to something, and I agreed.

I spent that night reflecting on that year, asking that Voice to guide my words and direct whatever it wanted to come out. I knew there were hurting hearts in the room and my heart was fixated on them. The next morning, on my way down to the conference, I met up with my friend Linda, who had asked to pray over me before I spoke. Not only did she pray over me, she anointed me with oils. I had never seen it done before, but embraced the gesture. I felt so honored in how she handled the moment that was before me. I loved the intentionality of it and the peace and power that came over me. I knew it was that Voice, ready to release an important message to the audience.

That morning, every second before I walked up on stage I was preparing my mind, speaking LIFE over it; speaking LIFE over my entire being. The moment my hands took the microphone, I shouted *"Behold!! He is doing a NEW thing!!!"* That was the theme Dani had been emphasizing so poetically all weekend, and here I was, living it out.

Jumping right into it, I shared how that very day, January 12, 2019 was not only the anniversary of my one-year of commitment to Dani's coaching, it was the 15th anniversary of the day we lost my dad to suicide: January 12th, 2004.

In that moment, I could feel all the hearts and the eyes

in the room were fixated on me, awaiting the next words that would come. Then I shared how I couldn't believe the LIFE the Father (the Voice) had brought me to, 15 years later!! I told them that, no matter where they were in their lives at that moment, it was not the end. Their story was not over. He has so much more in store for them!

I shared how, before coming to Dani's conferences, I was broke, frustrated, and deeply broken, and had no idea. I shared how that Voice had done amazing things in my life after tragedy, and led me to a life that others couldn't believe. Still, my heart knew there was more.

Reflecting over the last year under Dani's coaching, I shared the external results of epic gigs, debt being paid off, business tripling, and a team growing. But, I shared that it's not the external wins that were so moving to me, but rather the internal work on my heart. The father/daughter *"you can trust me"* message that Voice had shared so intimately with me. Then I shared the daydream, and how that Voice had so gently shown how He wanted me to simply take His hand. That He was a good dad, and I could trust Him.

After I shared the dream, I shared how there was also a story I had been afraid to tell. I shared about my virginity, and how the night before coming to that first event, I almost barreled head first toward death, but that

Voice had intervened and kept me on a track toward life. I shared that our coach and that community had been the vessel for His rescue.

Looking back on that day, what's crazy is that, as I shared, something totally came over me. It was as if my entire being was plugged into an outlet and was radiating power from within that was running through my veins. And I truly believe it was plugged into that Voice. Friend, I never imagined that 15 years later, on the very day of the anniversary of my dad's passing, I'd be on stage at a business conference sharing the epic-ness of what that Voice had done in the 15 years since his passing.

I have a hard enough time finding my car in a grocery store parking lot—do you think I could see this coming?! I had no idea that day was coming—even that weekend, let alone 15 years prior, when I thought my life was over. But my Rescuer was doing a NEW thing!

That day, I was beyond moved by what that Voice had done with my life, and how He had used so much pain to inspire hope into others who were hurting. After all, wasn't that the true desire of my heart? What a gift, to get to do that on the very anniversary!

After sharing all that, I can't even begin to list how many people came up to me and said how moved and inspired they were. So many shared with me that they, too, had lost someone to suicide or were suicidal themselves.

One woman in particular said something I'll never forget. She shared that she and her young daughter had just lost her husband (this young girl's father) to suicide just one year before. Her daughter had been barely paying attention to the conference all weekend, but the moment I shared that I had lost my dad to suicide, this little girl's head immediately shot up and started paying attention. This one story made my entire journey SO beyond worth it!! Knowing that it might have inspired this young little one was a major victory. Where she was at that moment was not the end for her, either. There were so many tears as this mom shared with me. THAT was a win for the whole team working that weekend, as well as for that Voice—the one that had rescued me and was still at work!

+++++

After that event, I learned that Bart, one of my dad's good buddies from the fire department, had been sharing my dad's story with different fire departments, trying to help others who might be dealing with the same issues.

I reached out to him and shared how moved I was to hear what he was doing with dad's story. Then I shared what had just happened on the 15th anniversary of dad's death, sharing his story with thousands. His response brought me to more tears. He was convinced we were saving lives with dad's story. As it turns out, he had spoken on the anniversary of dad's passing, too. How crazy is that?! Here we were, in different parts of the world, empowered to share the same message.

He also shared that, earlier that year, he had been given a chance to speak at his state's professional fire fighters union, and had asked that they make behavioral health in the fire profession a priority that next year. He sent photos of the engagement and shared that they had committed over six figures toward training and awareness, because of what he shared.

That Voice was up to way more than I had ever realized, and the rescue it intended to do was rippling in waves!

One day after that conference ended, our firm had a pre-scheduled video conference between our entire team and an important client (what am I saying? They're all important, and we love them all like family. But this client was larger than most at this time). We were given no context for why they desired to meet with our entire team, but happily waited, whatever the news was. Little did we know that this client was going to be presenting our firm with an award for being their 2019 "Vendor of the Year!" They had gone through all their vendors and reviewed who they felt was truly creative, thought outside the box, and genuinely cared about them. Needless to say, we were all stunned as they unveiled a glass-etched statue with our name.

Did I mention that our newly-hired project manager, Jenny had come with me to Dani's event, and it had been her very first one?!! She'd had a life-changing weekend of her own. She shared with me later, *"When you were on stage, I wanted to shout from the back of the room 'that's my boss'!!!!! I was so proud of you."*

Jenny wasn't someone new to my life, just new to our firm. We had known each other for years, having worked together many years prior at another company. What that Voice was doing within our rapidly-growing firm, my own heart, and Jenny...was another wave that was starting to ripple. She became a terrific leader for our team, leading us to new heights. She became an advocate for everything we were doing, but also for all that Voice was doing around her and within her, without even realizing it.

In fact, she probably didn't realize it until she read it here. But I want to take a minute to tell you, Jenny, that Voice has been at work in you, and He is doing a powerful thing within you and around you, and I am so proud of you. I am proud of what we are doing together, and what He is doing with us!

+++++

As I was eagerly awaiting my fast-approaching trip to the Holy Land, that Voice had more surprises for me.

The last ripple that hit before I left on that trip came with a call from a fire department from a city on the other side of the country. My mind raced as I wondered what this call could even be about, thinking, "*this must be something to do with dad, since he was a fireman.*" The fire chief on the call shared that he was going through applications on his desk and I was listed as a referral on one of them. He wondered if I would be willing to answer some questions. I had no idea this was coming, and my head and heart raced as I realized what it was, and who it was for: I was being asked to give a referral for the young woman who had shattered my heart.

I saw two roads ahead of me: I could have been totally justified in saying "*no*" to this chance, because I had felt lied to, played with, used, and betrayed. This friend had spewed some horrible words over me and some of the deepest wounds in my life. Granted, those were just MY feelings, and I needed to own them (versus blaming anyone for anything). But then I saw a second road: a road of honor, where I heard my coach's voice say, "*CHOOSE honor, help her to succeed.*" I knew this was the path a woman of high value—a daughter of the king—would take. I was being given a chance to speak LIFE about someone who had, in my mind, been associated with horrific wounds.

I chose the second road.

I spent over an hour on the phone, giving this friend a glowing and truthful recommendation. That fire chief would have been an idiot not to hire her with what I had shared. The truth was, I loved this friend deeply and thought the world of her, because she WAS an awesome person.

But she wasn't just an awesome person, she was one of the hardest workers I had ever known, with the biggest heart and desire to succeed. She always put her BEST into everything that she did and at times often underestimated how epic she truly was. She always believed there was better yet inside of her. This friend was (and is) the definition of a true fighter, a true champion. That's what I shared with this chief. Never in a million years did I think that I would be challenged to do that, but in forgiveness, I truly felt this friend's heart, and was able to do the impossible. I was able to help someone who I could have easily moved on from, forgotten, or said, *"no, she's the last one who deserves it, after how she dishonored me."* But that was exactly the point and the challenge I had been presented: would I honor the ones who had hurt me the most? Would I help them succeed? Interesting were the stories that Voice had been weaving, and this one felt like such a victory. It was a victory over me, over my own mind, and my own heart to help the hurting.

CHAPTER 19

"Just Take My Hand"

New Roots of Life in Israel

I was off to Israel!

The Holy Land. But to me, it wasn't just the Holy
Land. As I anticipated my feet touching the ground, it
was where I knew the spirit of that Voice—my Rescuer—
resided the most. The excitement within my spirit was
pulling me like a magnet right to where it belonged. I was
ready to feel that SNAP the moment our feet touched the
ground, and the moment we landed, I knew I was home.

Walking through the airport with our group, we
met up with Dani, who had arrived ahead of time, and
everything within me wanted to fall to my knees and

exclaim, *"Father, I am here!!!"*

Over the next 10 days, my heart went on a journey with that Voice that sent roots all the way down to the bedrock of my love for Him. That love had formed when I lost my earthly dad, and now, my experience of His presence in Israel wrapped around it and gave it new LIFE! Until this trip, I had never imagined that my love for that Voice could ever grow bigger. After walking through the loss of my dad, and discovering how present and powerful He was, I thought I had felt it all. But journeying to Israel took it to a whole new level. That Voice took my hand like a real father and delighted in showing me just how much He loved me everywhere I looked. It was as if He were right there beside me, walking with me everywhere we went, with everything that lit up my soul, saying *"Jen!!!! Jen!!!! Jen!!! Jen, do you see this!? Can you see that over there?!! Look at this!! Isn't that amazing!!? Do you see how much I love you?!!"*

That Voice was so powerful and so present the first few days, I was so overwhelmed by how much I was taking in. It actually felt like I was standing in front of a fire hose and someone was just blasting me right in the face with everything I ever wanted to know.

Intense, right?

I mean, have you ever been blasted in the face by a firehose? My whole life, I had grown up around the Bible. I had heard the stories my whole life, but I had always been embarrassed, because it all felt like a jumbled mess in my mind. I could never remember which people went with which story, in what order, let alone which details went to each one. I could only remember the major players: I knew Noah had an ark with two of every kind of animal, and there was a flood. But I couldn't remember the rest of the names or any more of the details of that event. And I had heard the stories my whole life!!

But here I was, in Israel, getting to SEE first-hand where these events took place, and learn details about each one. Going in order, taking in the sights, smelling the air, hearing the sounds, and touching the very ground where these stories took place. I quickly realized that the reason it had felt like a jumbled mess all these years was because I was a visual learner. It was like I was hearing it all for the first time (through a fire hose) with the massive amount of pages and pages of notes I was taking! I was capturing the experience the way I learn best.

The level of what was finally sinking in was so much that, by the third day, I was completely overwhelmed, but in a good way. As I wrestled to understand what was happening to me, that night I had a dream that so perfectly and poetically showed me what I was going through.

In the dream, our coach was sitting across from me, and I handed her a plate of food. As she took the plate, it tipped sideways and all the food slid off the plate. She reached down and picked up a piece of meat and threw it at me, and it smacked me right in the middle of the forehead. We both laughed hysterically. The next morning, I recalled the dream and *"what the heck was that about?"* That was weird. Were we going to have a food fight?! Would I get taken out first?! (I promise I have great aim. Have you seen me throw a gummi bear?) I shared the dream with others on the trip later that next day.

Then hit me: here I was, on this trip, being given the real "meat" of everything I believed. Everything that had been muddied up in my mind was getting scraped out and new clarity was hitting me right smack dab in the face. What that Voice did as He took me by the hand throughout Israel was the real meat my heart needed—the real journey He wanted to take me on.

Sometimes the Voice whispers, sometimes He cries out. In Israel, He shouts.

One of the first shouts came while we were visiting a place called Tel Arad. While I was there, it hit me: the timing of coming to Israel right after that entire first year of conferences with my coach couldn't have been more perfect. After a year of hard internal work, here I was,

enjoying the fruits of my labor in getting to simply be there. Not only had that year brought me to a place where I finally felt completely free, but it brought me closer to that Voice, and brought me to Israel, where I was getting to walk into the remains of the Holy of Holies, on Day One.

On my arms are tattoos that reach all the way up to my shoulders. Each mark represents a promise and a remembrance: the mountains from my time in Nevada, the year I spent getting "clean" because of being ALL-IN with events, my coach, and that Voice and the red stripe running through it all. What's even more interesting is that I hadn't asked the tattoo artist to do a red stripe, but something in me said to let him when he started. And here at the ruins of altar grounds at Tel Arad, I was learning that the blood that was shed on the altar was meant for cleansing. I bled—figuratively—all over that first year. My heart bled. And that blood was meant for restoring me more fully back to Him. I couldn't believe how that Voice had led me, right down to the very color of that red stripe on my arm. I was seeing the evidence of that Voice going before me again, as He had so many times before, in everything.

At times, I felt shame at what my heart had been cleansed of in that year. I learned at Tel Arad that "holy" didn't mean sinless, but rather, "set apart." We're not meant to feel shame, we're meant to cleanse! And we are cleansed by His blood. It's something we are suppose to do! In that moment, I felt more free, more loved, and my love for that Voice came to life even more.

I learned to pray there and to leave things behind. I dropped to the floor, so overwhelmed that He had led me there in that moment, by what He revealed.

As our whole group took a walk down the Road of the Patriarchs, the Voice whispered to me again. This is one of those roads traveled in ancient times by great people with names you would recognize. And as Dani gently dropped bits of wisdom along the way, every step I took I was overcome, speechless. *"Who was I, to be walking here?!!!"* In each step, heard him answer back, ***"YOU are worthy."***

At the end of the walk, Dani and two rabbis all shared messages. As they were speaking, something hit me. I had seen sheep everywhere we went in Israel, and Dani had been talking about the role of a shepherd. Honestly, we couldn't believe all the sheep we were seeing.

The two rabbi's shared how we had just been witnesses to actual Biblical prophecies that were being fulfilled today. One of them showed us the grapevines near his house and how his son had eaten a grape from one, fulfilling an ancient prophecy.

We visited the Cave of the patriarchs (where Abraham, Isaac, Leah, Rachael, Adam, and Eve are all buried); and Dani gathered us all together in a tight huddle to pray a blessing over us. She prayed for the blessing of Abraham to be passed to us. In that act, she was literally being a good shepherd of the flock she was guiding. Pretty crazy for all the sheep we were seeing!

I prayed on the floor that day. I asked that Voice for influence, and to be bold like so many other men we had been learning about on this trip. I wanted to be bold like Dani, who was praying next to me. As I looked to the future, all I could think was, *"That Voice is with us! This is it. Game on."* I couldn't wait to see what that Voice would do with that fulfillment. The prayer that started on Day One of our trip, was the prayer that Voice laid on my heart all week, everywhere we went. That Voice gave me a deep compassion to see people's lives restored around the world.

The prayer continued at Mt Nebo. I learned the significance of Moses being there, and the view he saw (knowing that the Promise Land was ahead of him, but he would never enter in). As Dani had us listen to the words of Dr. Martin Luther King, Jr., my heart was again led to pray for others. As I soaked in that view for myself, I prayed for the broken people that Voice would someday lead me to. I prayed to speak in the same way that Dr.

King spoke for freedom of his people. I prayed for the broken to be freed from their land of bondage, whatever that might be. I asked that He would go before me and prepare their hearts in advance, and that He would give me the revelation of the words when I need them.

Alongside such a powerful moment of prayer, I realized I had been given a personal association to every story I knew from the Bible as we visited each place. They were no longer stories from the past. That same Voice that spoke to them was speaking to me, in the same way that He spoke to them, in the same places. The Bible was coming alive.

As we were challenged to think about our own "Egypt," and what was holding us back (or keeping us trapped), I realized mine was thinking that I wasn't qualified, I wasn't worthy, and I wasn't good enough. How could it be me?

That Voice softly answered, *"I qualify you. You are more than enough. I made you exactly as I intended to: for a purpose, for a people, to set those people free. I will equip you. I will speak boldly through you. I will empower you through every cell of your body to fulfill the vision I have for you. Stand up and fight for them with your voice. You are ready. You are chosen. Stay humble. Seek me. Seek me with all of your heart, as you are now.*

Your shepherds (both Me and your earthly one) see it, in you. And we are cheering you on, standing beside you, believing for victory. Victory in the hurting."

CHAPTER 20

"I'm So Proud Of You"

Unearthing Even More

As we continued our adventure through Israel, not only was that Voice speaking loudly to me, it was as if He was unearthing desires within me that I didn't know were even there. As He was bringing the Bible to life around me, He was bringing things to life within me!

At the ruins of the walls of Jericho, as Dani read the story from the Bible, something within me stirred and said, "I want that!" Chills ran through my whole being, as I realized that Rahab had married into the line of one who loved God the most. It revealed a desire within me that I didn't even know I had. That Voice was uncovering my desire. His desires.

Before attending my first conference, I had ZERO desire to get married, but that had changed over time while watching what Dani and her husband, Hans were giving to the world. My visit to Israel (especially at Jericho) uncovered more of that desire. Dani shared about the significance of circling something seven times, and how the Israelites circled the walls of Jericho seven times before the walls fell.

The number seven symbolizes completion. Suddenly, I felt like my head exploded with revelation! I knew in that moment that Voice had just uncovered another desire, which played like a movie in my mind: the desire to circle my spouse seven times at my own wedding someday, to symbolize the completion of my heart's journey.

I had no idea if that was a thing, but in that moment, I wanted to do it! I thought I had a vision for something unique to do someday. But later that week, I was invited to attend a marriage renewal for a couple in our group. Dani was officiating and I stood near her. She turned to the bride and said, *"I want you to circle your groom seven times."*

I was stunned. WAIT! People actually do this?!?!! I had discovered a new desire within my own heart, and here it was lived out in front of me. How amazing is that, for the gentle leading of a father?! Had I seen that or even voiced to anyone what I envisioned before He uncovered my desire for it, it wouldn't have meant as much. That Voice was powerfully going before me, and making sure that I saw that He was.

Leaving Jericho that day, I wrote this in my journal:

"Wouldn't it be great if my heart never feared loss, because it was completely filled by Him? Wouldn't it be great if I was qualified? If I was worthy? I was good enough? Wouldn't it be great if it were me? Wouldn't it be great if I were equipped to speak to the broken, to the masses— just like Dr. King?

Wouldn't it be great if he gave me inspired words that were just as powerful? ...just as memorable? ...just as world-changing? ...so that not my words, but His words are remembered as my legacy? Wouldn't it be great if my coach, my dad, and—someday—that Voice looked at me and said, 'I knew you were going to be doing THIS and I saw it in you the first day I laid eyes on you...and here we are now, and I'm seeing it fulfilled." And not only was it fulfilled, but was done while honor radiated from you to your coach, to your battles, your enemies, to your world, and, most importantly, to that Voice.

"Wouldn't it be great if I went into every battle with the 10 commandments on my heart? If I was transparent as to what was leading me and every one of my words?

"Wouldn't it be great if every battle were won because of that Voice, and my reliance on His simple instructions and His power in each one? Wouldn't it be great if I was known as a shepherd, and someday...a king?"

Friend, have you ever asked yourself, "what if?" What if there were nothing stopping you, nothing holding you back, and anything were possible?

What would you do?

+++++

As amazing as that experience was at Jericho, what happened at Shiloh was even better.

That Voice continued to unearth things deep within me. When we got off the bus at Shiloh, Dani said to me, **"You're going to love Shiloh".** Little did I know how much I would love it and what that Voice would do with my own heart there.

At Shiloh, we watched a video of the story of what had happened there: how Hannah prayed for a son, and how her prayer was answered. As I watched the video, I heard the words, ***"I'm so proud of you,"*** and started to cry. My coach had said those words to me only days before. I thought of my dad, and how proud he would have been to see what his daughter was doing. How proud he would have been to hear that I was in Shiloh, walking in the place where prophecy and promises were being fulfilled in real time.

Then I realized that the Bible isn't stories of the past, it's alive and being fulfilled today!! I suddenly realized that we are living the Bible right now! We are literally a part of it.

But then it hit me hard... *"If only dad knew what he was rooted to, that HE was a part of prophecy in being led here, too, not long before he died."* Tears streamed down my face. And as the group exited the movie and we moved over to another part of the grounds, I lagged behind, because I was just completely breaking down emotionally. Dani challenged everyone to take some time to themselves. I went and found a spot by myself and fell to the ground and wept. I ugly-cried, sobbing with snot dripping from my nose. I wept for all those who were dying not knowing their roots. All those who were dying not knowing how LOVED and valued they are by that Voice!

I was broken by His Vision for me. But then I felt the

significance of Him breaking me there: it was the very
same place where Hannah's heart was broken, she prayed,
and her heart's prayer was fulfilled. As I walked back
to the bus and looked over the fields—the fields full of
promises fulfilled—I heard that Voice say, ***"I am going to
fulfill promises like this in your life, Jen."***

I surely did not doubt that He would.

+++++

Our next stop was En Gedi. It's literally an
unbelievably beautiful oasis and a nature reserve in Israel,
west of the Dead Sea. It's also one of the pivotal places in
the story of the battles between David and Saul. A place
where David was inspired to write many of the Psalms.
En Gedi got me thinking more about shepherds and how
sheep follow shepherds. It got me thinking about my life,
the shepherd I had been given, and how grateful I was.

At En Gedi, Dani challenged us: *"what will be birthed
NEW in your life?"* Knowing that Voice just wanted us to
listen, I shot up a quick silent prayer: *"Yahaveh (His name
in Hebrew), give me revelation for however you want to
use me in influence."* What blew me away was that, while
I couldn't wait to study that Voice further, I hadn't even
started trekking further through the Oasis there—which
we would be doing next on our own—and that voice was
already revealing, speaking through the creation all around

me.

As I took each step, venturing and winding my way through the caves, waterfalls, and mountains of En Gedi I heard:

"I will lay out every STEP before you. You don't need to worry; they will be in PLAIN SIGHT. The distractions will be like PEBBLES around you; they will not keep you from your PATH. You will barely even notice them; they will feel so minor in comparison that you will laugh at them.

"You will come upon STREAMS of life on your journey. I will give you VIEWS ahead along the journey that will seem more beautiful than you can imagine. It may appear like everything is about to FALL, but don't worry: it is secure—there is a FOUNDATION you cannot see. It will not tumble into ruin. It will stand strong, a beautiful symbol of My presence and My promise.

"There will be CUTS—deep wounds—CREVACES of pain, and enemies that will try to pierce you, but they will not. You are grounded in Me. Even these attacks will appear like beautiful lines that mark your journey. There will even be treasures inside of some of the holes the attacks have left. You will have shepherds/leaders go before you that you can trust

not to lead you astray."

Suddenly, I saw my coach on the path just ahead of me. The message continued:

"Some steps will feel unsteady, but just hold on to Me. You will find shade and rest in the OVERGROWTH, in the stops along your journey, where new life has sprung forth. They will bless you, but don't stay there. There is more for you. It may look like you're supposed to turn down another PATH, but don't go there—it only leads to RUIN, to a dead-end.

"There will be distractions, like boulders on your journey. Don't let them stop you, distract you, or impede the FLOW. It may get even more intense, but press on. The more you do, the more you will see what's coming.

"There will be TWISTS and TURNS. I will give life from ABOVE. There will be several sources for life, but I will make it DISTINCT which you should drink from. I will be your safety when the path gets slippery.

"It may get completely DARK, but just keep walking. I will lead you to ABUNDANCE. The crows will try to come feed off your abundance. Will you stop to feed the hungry? It might seem easier to

continue they way you've been living, but I'm calling you to a different path. The path might seem more difficult—even dangerous—but you will soon be on paved ground, where you will be able to walk securely, enjoy the fruit, the view, and the people.

"Be aware that in that new land, trees that you have always thought were healthy will need to be UPROOTED because they don't fit in this new land. In the end will be the sounds of CELEBRATION, of voices mixing from various languages. A sea of cultures. All in my SHADE."

That Voice was weaving a message with every step I took in ways that felt poetic.

As we then walked through the city of David, our guide read the story of King David. He was a mighty King, but he had some pretty big failures in his life. But he didn't try to hide what he had done. That touched me. That moved me. That inspired me. I mean, come on—how many of us, when we mess up, tell the whole world? No, most of the time, we hide our failures and we hope no one ever finds out. We put them in a locked box and swallow the key. Heck, we put the key we swallowed into a puzzle box that only a brilliant mind could open, then we put it in a maze, and booby trap it up the wazoo. Ain't nobody going to find THAT out! But David royally messed up and he wrote about it?! And we're still reading about his mess up to this day, AND he's referred to as one who loved God the most? How crazy is that? How radical is that? What faith he had in the one he loved the most.

I was so moved about the importance and power of transparency, knowing that I had felt that Voice leading me toward sharing my whole story. As I walked along the tunnels and ruins beneath the grounds, it hit me: I had been responsible for feeding the current desires of my heart, whether that was from being exposed to others choices, or because of my own choices.

+++++

Later that day we toured the tunnels of Hezekiah under Jerusalem. While I was there, the Voice showed me how much I was loved. Back in Jericho, this Voice had uncovered my heart's true desires—desires I didn't even know I had. But in the tunnels of Hezekiah, as our guide described how the Earth was revealing things that had been buried for centuries all around Israel, I was struck by how LOVED we were to even be there at that moment. To be a part of the ones this Voice had called back to Israel. I fought the tears as His overwhelming love came over me.

As we walked out into the pouring rain, our guide confirmed that we were walking the same ground Yeshua (Jesus) walked on. I lost it even more. I heard that Voice say, *"There is nothing that will keep you from hearing how much I love you right now—not wind, not rain, not cold. You were called here and I am with you!"* He was unearthing things within me that He had put there for me to discover. It was just one more way He was showing me just how much He loved me. And I hope you realize by now He wants to do the same for you.

CHAPTER 21

"*I See You*"

Filling Every Single Crack

As we neared the tail of our journey, our whole group visited the Sea of Galilee. We boarded a ship just like the disciples did back in Biblical times. Out on the water, as I stared across the sea from the side of the boat with the sea breeze on my face, it hit me that this was where the disciples learned to trust that Voice, and here I was, learning the same thing on the same sea.

The ship's crew played a few songs over the ship's speakers. As the worship song, *It Is Well*, blasted, I lost it again, recalling how powerful those words and message had been in the days (and years) after dad's passing. A Jewish friend, Hadassah, who had been on the trip with us, saw me tearing up and whispered, *"He is going to use you mightily, Jen."* I continued to cry as I looked out at the sea, the wind blowing on my face, and the song drifting over the ship. In that moment, I felt my own heart say, *"I am ready."*

Hadassah told me to remember the verse, John 14:12:

"Truly, truly, I say to you, he who believes in Me, the works that I do he shall do also. And greater works than these He shall do, because I go to My Father"

She continued, *"I always wondered, what is GREATER than healing the sick, casting out demons, and so on? He is going to use you MORE than that, Jen."*

How did this friend know that?! It didn't matter how. I was so aware of that presence of that Voice as I sailed that sea that I didn't doubt that He loved me, saw me in that moment, and spoke. I knew, looking back on my whole journey, that whatever this Voice was going to do, He would finish what He started.

I'll never forget that moment.; it is etched permanently in my heart.

+++++

Later, Dani took us to have lunch with a group of

orphans and widows we had been helping through Kings Ransom Foundation, a nonprofit charity that gives 100% of what's donated to the poor. Prior to finding that organization, I had never heard of ANY organization that operated that way. Their operating expenses are fully underwritten by a private corporate sponsor. After a year of donating to King's Ransom, here I was, seeing the faces of the very people we had been helping. It broke me. I watched as Dani spoke to them through a translator, thinking, *"She has the heart of the Father."* I remember being so thankful for how hard she fought for the poor and the forgotten.

The Voice had given me a vision for the kind of woman I want to be: one who loves that Voice more than anything, and because of that Voice could do more for OTHERS. Dani was the first person I had ever been able to look at and say, *"SHE gives a vision that reflects how big I know my God is."* In that moment, I knew I could never say thank you enough for what she was modeling to me through her life.

That day, we got to eat lunch with these amazing people. I got to be face-to-face with a woman with two young daughters who had just lost their dad to suicide. While we couldn't understand each other's spoken words, I could tell by the cast of her face and mine that our spirits connected. This woman held my face in her hands, with tears in her eyes, and then reached out for an embrace, and I knew that He had delivered something powerful. Friend, if I could have ever chosen a place where the depths of my heart could make an impact, this would be it: to people with hurting hearts. That Voice had led me here at this moment on this day.

As we drove back to the hotel, that Voice had more to say. Our tour guide was sharing about the orphans and widows in the city of Migdal Ohr, he mentioned that, in Israel an "orphan" is a child with only one parent.

The moment he said that, my heart skipped a beat and exclaimed, *"HE SEES ME!!!"* It wasn't his design for a child to lose a parent. That's why I had always felt like I had been abandoned, and it was up to me to figure it all out; why I felt like I had fallen through the cracks, and it was up to me to fight to get out. That was why I had been so driven my whole life. But in that moment, it was so freeing to hear what an orphan really was. For the first time, I felt seen. I don't mean that, up until that point He hadn't seen me. What I mean is, I felt like that Voice showed me right then, that He saw another deep crack in my heart—that He saw them all!

Before the trip was over, that Voice had one more powerful message to share. Dani talked about the Hebrew roots of many things in our culture today: Mr. Spock (from Star Trek), many superheroes, and even the letter 'W' in Wonder Woman have roots in Hebrew culture. I had no idea until that day!! As I looked down at the tattoo sleeve on my arm, on the inside of my upper arm, I have a Wonder Woman form in the shape of a tree, coming out of water, and with a slingshot in her hands like King David. I put this Wonder Woman-esque tree there because I felt like she symbolized a modern-day warrior fighting battles. It wrapped three verses together for me, as a reminder to be a warrior of the flow of that Voice, to speak life, and (hopefully) I would be remembered someday as an oak of righteousness in it. Little did I know that even the Wonder Woman nod was from biblical/Hebrew roots!!! Now I had evidence, that all of these things I had done had been inspired by that Voice.

What a way for that Voice to end the journey He had just taken me on: as a Father, reminding me of the warrior He had been developing inside me my whole life.

CHAPTER 22

"You Were Born With The Gift Of Faith"

Breaking Free From Me

Coming home from Israel, I was ready to face some battles, both professionally and personally, but wow, did I feel equipped! My trust in that Voice was through the roof, and I'm glad it was. Without that faith, I wouldn't have been able to walk in the battles that arose almost immediately.

I was hired pretty much immediately for another gig. The gig was going to be for two-and-a-half months—the longest one by far I had ever been a part of, and absolutely at that budget level of production in the entertainment industry. I was hired to work for a very successful and well-known show that was in its 19th & 20th seasons.

I was thrilled, but as pre-production started, I realized very quickly it would be the most challenging gig I had ever experienced. In just the few weeks of prep before shooting even started, I was so overwhelmed, I battled tears and thoughts of, *"how is THIS even possible, in this timing?!"* That Voice was not only with me, there's no doubt in my mind it also went before me.

As we started, I was so overwhelmed that I got to a place where I knew that all I could do was make the choice every day to:

- show up, and do the best I can
- have the best attitude with everyone that I meet

That way, if they fired me, or it ended for some reason, I could know I did the best I could. I knew that "tomorrow" was out of my hands, and I leaned back into the arms of that Voice, knowing that no matter what happened, He had me. I couldn't have done any of the days of that gig without that Voice. The two weeks I had just spent in Israel laid an incredible foundation of trust I know I needed to take such a leap of faith.

That gig proved to be the most challenging and intense pressure I had ever been in. As the gig came to a close,

I could see the evidence of my coach's influence and the presence of that Voice as I reflected on several comments:

"Jen, I haven't heard ONE complaint about you or your department."

"I love coming to graphics; every time I open the door, there you are with a huge smile on your face to greet me... it's such a delightful contrast."

It would be easy to say, *"That was just you, Jen. That's who you are."* Sure, but at the same time, would that have been me at THIS level of stress and insanity? I'd be lying if I said yes. It's no joke, many quit or were fired. It was the most intense environment and opportunity I had ever been in. So, to have these kinds of remarks within that environment was just as shocking to me as it might be to you. But I truly believe that was the impact of an amazing coach who had been speaking into me for over a year.

That first professional battle after my trip to Israel had been won. That one huge gig led to several more gigs that same year at the same level. I wish I could tell you the names of the shows—or the production companies names—but I can't. You'd know them, though. What I can say is, everything He did with the first 14 years of this journey doesn't hold a candle to what He did in the fifteenth year. But like I said, it wasn't just the professional battles that I faced upon returning home; there were personal battles as well.

During that two-and-a-half month gig, I still attended every conference that happened.

Wait…how, Jen? If you were working 12-hour days six days a week, how did you go to two weekend conferences in another state with your coach? Before taking the gig, I had negotiated it into the deal, basically saying that I had a previous commitment, and that if they were okay with a proxy (a sub) during those weekends, then I'd be happy to take the gig. Plus, I was ready to walk away if they said no. With everything that Voice and this coach had been doing in my life, there was no way I was going to miss an event. I was ALL-IN. And I knew that the more success came, the harder it could become to stay the course, so I had already made my decision. Thankfully, they said that wouldn't be a problem, and I attended two conferences amidst the insanity of that production.

I'm so glad I did.

Each of the conferences brought different lessons: for example, I learned how to set boundaries and keep a healthy work balance in my life. But I'll never forget what happened at my third leadership event. We were challenged to choose how we were going to speak life over ourselves and what we were going to CHOOSE to believe. What came out of me I believe came from that Voice.

I wrote, *"Jen, you ARE so loved. You are highly valuable. We have become so intimate. I am so proud of you. Your dad is proud of you. Choose to believe that you are lovable, loved, and will not be rejected. Choose to believe the impossible is possible and will happen. Choose to believe I already have it all planned out for you and nothing is a mistake. Choose to believe I will redeem it all. Choose to believe that where I want to take you is just beginning. Choose to believe you are seen. Choose to believe you're not invisible. Choose to believe juicy fruit is coming! Choose to believe that your sprouts are producing a tree that will be SO BIG!! Choose to believe the roots we set in Israel were planted in GOOD soil. Choose to believe, trust, and now watch me. Here we go my daughter".*

What a gift those words were! Had I not been there, I would have missed out on that message from the Voice. I also would have missed out on what came next.

That same evening, there was a more intense spiritual session, and countless people in the room were getting set free from things that were holding them back. Sitting in the front row, I had been keeping my eyes closed during the entire session because I had wanted both my heart and mind to be completely focused on that Voice, whatever else might be happening in the room for others. I wanted to be in tune with what He was doing with me. As Dani walked through the room and prayed over different people, all of a sudden, I could tell she was standing right in front of me. I knew because the moment I sensed she was there, she put a hand on my shoulder, thumped a Bible against my gut, and proceeded to pray over me so intensely that tears were streaming down her face. The first words that came out of her were, *"I pray against the spirit of fear."* Dani then "went to town," praying over me, FIGHTING for me. As she said, *"you will NOT take this one,"* two things happened that I'll never forget.

The more she prayed, the more I felt a sensation inside my chest, around my heart. My heart was getting physically warm—I could feel the temperature rising, to the point that I vividly remember thinking, *"Holy crap, my heart is so HOT right now!! What is happening to me?!"* As I shared that sensation later with my friend Hadassah, she said, *"Jen, He was burning something OFF of you, off of your heart!"* The moment she said that, it confirmed what had happened.

I remember picturing the superhero called Spawn! You know how he has all this black gunk that just sticks to everything and wraps itself around the guy and, no matter what he does, he can't get it off, it just has a life of it's own? As Dani prayed and my heart got hotter, that's what I saw! I saw this black, tar-like gunk that had been wrapped all around my heart, suddenly set ablaze until it completely burned off of me!

Crazy, right?!

Something epic had absolutely happened, and there's no doubt in my mind that something BAD had been burned off of me. I could actually physically feel that it had happened.

The second thing that I'll never forget from that moment is how insanely loved I felt. As Dani stood there, right in front of me, going to town, FIGHTING for my very life, I was so moved. Who does that?! In that moment, she showed me the high value that was marked on my life. Someone thought I was WORTH going to BATTLE for!!! No matter what anyone else thought of her in that moment, she went to battle for me. She showed me, in physical form, how that Voice—the Father—felt about me: I was worth fighting for!!! And in that moment, I continued to see the leader I desired to be for others. She was that leader for me, in her own heart for others.

Friend, can you imagine what I would have missed if I had not been there THAT weekend?! Now turn it around: imagine what would happen if we went to BATTLE for others like that! I think we'd hit homeruns all over the place.

+++++

Later that summer came another huge victory: a victory over me. The timing also proved to be interesting. Dani was going through a battle of her own, a battle of loss. She had lost someone she deeply loved. Not only did she not cancel the event, she came and gave 100% of herself for the people in the room. Had she not come, I would have missed out on another miracle.

On the first day of this conference, she said, ***"You were BORN with the gift of faith-what are you doing with it?"*** Something clicked inside of me. I could feel my spirit reply, ***"YESSSSSS! Jen...this is you!!!"***

As she asked, *"what needs to change in you?"* I finally realized I needed to get out of my own way. I needed to STOP listening to my own heart, and listen JUST to that Voice—to Him. My heart had been confused and I didn't know how to get out of that confusion, but I didn't need to know how. I just needed to listen for His voice above all else.

As I continued to diligently seek Him, He would continue to speak, reveal Himself, and light the way— gently, as a Father, just as He had been on this whole last year and a half with my coach. I needed to fully embrace my gift of faith in EVERY area of my life! I knew people looked at my story—in fact, I even looked at my own story—as a story of great faith in how big our God is, but it was like I was operating in 95% faith, and it hadn't occurred to me until that weekend. That 5% I was missing was because of the old problem in my mind, telling me that *"my heart, in regards to love, is confused."*

It hit me like a ton of bricks in that moment that I had been listening to my OWN voice, my OWN heart, and my OWN mind, instead of just looking to Him! All along, He had been subtly and softly speaking to me as a GOOD father leading me forward, one step at a time, revealing desires within me that I didn't even know that I had. I needed to stop saying, *"I'm confused."* I needed to stop listening to my own heart and just listen to that Voice with great faith! I needed to throw out that old program.

For the first time in my life, I wrote down a specific vision for my marriage. I had gotten specific with my mind and heart over a year and a half, but now I was getting specific with my marriage. My dream included:

- A marriage that would be passionate about sharing the love of that Voice with the hurting. Traveling the world, adventuring all over, and loving on people. Iron sharpening iron, with my best friend.

- Voices together boldly radiating him.

- Believing in the impossible. Becoming a couple seen as ones living that out, as people exclaim "Yea, that's them!"

- Continuing to stay humble.

- Focusing on others, helping to raise them up, drawing out their potential and gifting.

- Seeing their eyes light up as that Voice awakens them. Awakens their spirit. Lights explode all over the world as we become known as vessels together helping that Voice set His people free!

Wow! I cannot wait for that.

Dani has often said, ***"a man without a vision will perish."*** When she said that, it struck me that the Voice had been giving me a vision to pursue. And that as I focus on it, I'm giving it life. He was giving me a sneak peek so that I would have faith. Because He is fighting for me.

There was a powerful woman who shared her story from the stage that weekend. Afterward, we ended up with a beautiful moment to chat on a quick session break, as we were both sitting in the front row. I poured life into her, thanked her for her courage in sharing, and described the amazing gift she had just given to the whole audience. She started to sob and then shared more. She described the rejection she's had to face along her journey and how being bold has opened her up to massive resistance. She shared how she had to fight through thoughts of "is it worth it?"

I was able to repeat something Dani had said that weekend: *"It will be messy! But surround yourself with people who will encourage you to do it, because there were people in the audience that needed to hear your voice and your message. THAT's who it is meant for!"*

This amazing woman asked me to pray over her just as Dani began to speak from the stage. But knowing that the Voice was continuing to work in that moment, even though that moment was for her, it was interesting how her battle spoke to my spirit. Her story of embracing her boldness and facing down rejection helped more things click in my mind, with my own story. It's so crazy to me how much that Voice works in those around us, how intricately He weaves His love and the things He wants us to hear. Even positioning us at a place and a moment to hear them.

I can't imagine my life if I hadn't been at that conference. But boy, was I thankful it had, that our coach and that community of people continued to take a RISK for others—even when their hearts were hurting. They were fighting their own battles and struggling for growth and breakthroughs in their own journeys. That Voice was doing a new thing, and the light to the path ahead was getting even brighter.

CHAPTER 23

"You Were Never Meant To Carry This"

A Giant Tree Falls

In the same way I'll never forget January of 2018, I'll also never forget November of 2019.

While attending my fourth leadership conference, I had an experience that I believe culminates the entire journey of this book. Something had grown in my life that I had been completely blind to. The Voice was so intentional with how it led me through the conference—again like a gentle father—revealing a brokenness in my heart.

Heading into that weekend I was hit with the news that my college mentor, who had helped me walk through tragedy, had tragically lost her husband. He left behind four kids, all around the same age I was when I lost my dad. I carried their grief on my mind and heart the next day. I knew what they were going through. I was walking to my mailbox when I vividly heard that Voice say to me, ***"Keep walking...I've got this!"***

I was given a chance to rule my own spirit, as I watched a family that I deeply loved walk through the same kind of pain. I could have stayed home and mourned, I suppose. But I chose to go to the conference. I imagined myself under the flow of a waterfall, washing away the burden and pain. In Israel, they call it a mikvah. It's a powerful experience, if you ever get the chance. I was preparing myself to hear whatever the Voice wanted me to that weekend. I had no idea how huge and vital that decision would be.

I "ended up" sitting next to a man who was my very first "line buddy" at my very first event (in the front row). Here we were, two years later, reflecting on how much we had changed. I viewed him as an amazing father who loved his family. He had made my own eyes well up with tears as he spoke of the love he had as a father. I highly respect him, and I know how much he loves that Voice. He reminded me of the heart of my own father.

I realized in the absence of my father, fear had taken

root in my heart and had grown into a giant tree. As I sat next to this tremendous father figure that I admired so much, I realized that giant tree of fear was being ripped up by the roots and falling down.

That day, we did an exercise identifying the "fruit" in our lives—the thought and behavior patterns we exhibited in our daily activities. She directed us to focus on one and trace it to the root. That's when I had a major breakthrough that I believe changed everything.

I identified the fruit of feeling like I had to prove myself. How many times had I been devastated when a gig fell through?

As I traced that fruit to it's root, this thought came up:

"Why do you feel like you need to prove yourself, Jen?"

A reply seemed to bubble up from the core of my heart: *"Because I have to show that my dad's death doesn't define the rest of my life!"*

"Why?"

"Because he gave up. I can't give up. I can't show people that their life isn't worth it."

"Why?"

"Because if I do, people will die!"

"Why are you carrying this responsibility Jen?"

"Because, what if I could have done something?! Dad wouldn't have died!"

What?! I never even knew these thoughts were in there!! I had forgiven my dad...but I hadn't forgiven ME! I hadn't forgiven myself, and it twisted a nasty bed of roots in the core of my heart.

Only days before, Dani had challenged me to write this book. I broke out into a complete sweat so bad that my entire body was sweating all the way down to my legs. No really, you could have licked my legs like a popsicle with how bad I was sweating. I didn't stop sweating for the next 4 hours. I was terrified to be that exposed and vulnerable with myself, let alone you. But that challenge from her, was exactly what I needed—this book wouldn't be in your hands had that not happened. This breakthrough at this event wouldn't have happened if I hadn't just started writing.

I had just begun writing the part about seeing my dad in his casket for the first time. I saw myself standing there about 10 feet away, completely frozen. I couldn't move. As I recalled that moment, it hit me that I never let myself say goodbye. I was too frozen and stunned. I walked myself through confessing the moment, forgiving it, and releasing it, saying:

> "*I forgive you, Jen, for thinking there was something you could have done!! I forgive you, Jen, for thinking you weren't good enough for him to stay. I forgive you, Jen, for not saying goodbye. I forgive you, Jen, for not wanting to let him go!*"

As those last two lines came out, I completely choked up. I couldn't catch my breath. I started to ugly cry as the rest of the words came out. I never knew I needed to say those words to myself. I had been carrying that all these years!!!

In that moment, I saw a major bad tree in my heart collapse and shatter to the ground. Physically I felt so much lighter!! A major weight I had been carrying around all these years was lifted off of me. I felt free. Every time I thought about that moment the whole weekend tears came. I was so touched by how that Voice had led me into the weekend, gently nudging me to give it to Him. He had led me into a safe place, sitting next to a beautiful example of an earthly Father. He helped me identify that root through Dani's training just days before.

At one point later that weekend, a guest speaker picked me out of the audience to use in a demonstration. He blindfolded me and had people lead me around until I no longer knew where I was in the room. He then asked Dani to come on stage and direct me through a crowded room with nothing but voice commands.

In that demonstration, He showed me what He had been doing all along. I was being led by a Voice. I allowed myself to be led blindly by the coach I trusted, loved, and admired. She led me all the way up to the stage—to freedom! It was a metaphor for the whole weekend; really, for the whole two years! I found more freedom than I ever could have imagined there would be. That Voice continues to lead me with the same words He said in the very beginning, *"we got this, Jen, you and Me."*

So many tears, but these were the good tears. He is so good!!! He had done far more than I could imagine, and was continuing to do it.

That moment changed everything. It changed the heart of the woman you've been reading along with this whole book, who felt like she HAD to help the hurting and the broken. It set my heart free. I had been carrying the weight of the world on my shoulders, and hadn't even realized it! I no longer felt the pressure of what I HAD to do, and instead only felt what I WANTED to do. I let go of the feeling that, unless I accomplished this massive future goal to help thousands of hurting hearts, I would have failed. That feeling was replaced with peace and rest that the burden of it wasn't on me. It was no longer about a massive future goal; it was about continuing to be present in every single moment, seeking that Voice within every moment, and finding Him in every one.

After that leadership conference, that epic internal victory rippled out to the rest of my life. I could only chuckle as I reflected on it. My company had a team up in New York City, shooting our very first video production, while two others managed two huge clients in the Midwest. In Las Vegas, I worked with another designer on a series of giant wall graphics that were going to be going up in a very well-known studio in Los Angeles. We were designing them for a brand new TV show that would premiere in the spring (interesting note: we hung these wall graphics over the set of an existing hit TV show that was on hiatus). And this all happened while I "sat in my office," which was the corner of my living room in the desert in Nevada. And here, I thought I wasn't a "businesswoman." Hah! So crazy the boxes and the limits we put ourselves in.

But as I sat in my living room that day and chuckled at how much my own mindset and reality had changed, I couldn't have been more thankful for who my coach was, the impact she already had on my life, and what that Voice had been doing amidst it all. But that wasn't even all of it.

As we neared the holidays, I decided that I was going to fly home to spend time with my immediate family. We hadn't been speaking for about five years, but now that things were healing, I wanted to be intentional about spending time with them. My niece and nephew heard that I was coming home before I even told them and burst into my mom's home in Michigan, saying, *"Aunt Jen is coming home just to see us!!"* I could have cried. For five years I wasn't allowed to see them. They were my buddies; I loved them!! Getting to hear how excited they were, seeing my family heal, there were no words for how grateful I was. Grateful to my coach, and grateful to that Voice. He restores!!

CHAPTER 24

"You Choose"

Where Do I Go From Here?

So, where do you go from here?

I know where I'm going: I'm going to continue looking and listening for that VOICE in everything. I know there's so much more that Voice still wants to do! Who knows? There may even be a whole other book ready in another 15 years, as that Voice continues to work. I wouldn't doubt it for one second!

My friend, Linda posted a photo of herself bungee jumping in South Africa, but this wasn't just any old photo. I couldn't stop staring at it because it symbolized so much more to me than just a fun moment. I knew this woman as a friend and a leader. In the photo she's not just jumping; her body is completely horizontal in the air, arms outstretched, reaching to the sky, head UP with the biggest smile on her face. She looks like she has zero fear, like she was BORN to do what she was doing. This was who she was. She had been completely set free, but didn't stay stagnant in that freedom.

She continues to LEAP with 100% of her heart for more—more for herself, her family, and hearts around the world. She's blazing a trail for the rest of us just by how she CHOOSES to face every single day. She is leading more people than she even realizes just by being who she is and continuing to press further into who He created her to be! That's a woman of courage. That's a woman with fight. That's a woman showing all of us that every single day—every single moment—is worth it!

My friend, what if we had THAT kind of courage to face every single moment of our lives—to not just face our fears, but to leap at them, with no assurance of whether we might fall? What would happen? I can tell you this: You're not going to find out if you don't leap! I, for one, can't think of a better approach to the rest of this life than to be ALL-IN.

Success in anything comes with failures. Just ask any of the "greats." Do you know how many times NBA

star Michael Jordan failed before he succeeded? FAIL
FORWARD! Fail with your entire being! Fail forward and
have fun with it! JUMP into the unknown!

These words are for me as I write this. I know the
Voice that's taken me this far has so much MORE he
wants to show me, and it's that Voice that I will be looking
for!

If you want someone to hold you accountable, I know
an amazing coach. This coach will continue to call out
the leaper in you! No one will get it perfect 100% of the
time—heck, sometimes we'll even get caught forgetting
to fully leap! I know I have. But this coach will hold you
accountable and, like she did with me, remind you of who
you are and who you were designed to be, and get you right
back to putting 100% effort into the jump! Do it messy! Do
it afraid! Just do it!

Did you know that King David, before he was a king,
was a shepherd? And when a giant came, and no one
wanted to fight him, David not only volunteered, he RAN
toward Goliath? I had never seen that before. Re-reading
the story, it hit me: David RAN toward Goliath?! He ran
toward his fear?! He didn't just even face his fear, he ran
toward it!!!

Are you ready, friend? Are you ready to step up, rise

up, and do something great with your life? Let's be a people who run toward everything we face in life! I believe in you!

Friend, this entire book you've been reading about that Voice, how I found it and you've been reading about the vessels that Voice used to speak into that journey. You've read countless of stories of how he used that coach. I can't imagine everything she has had to fight through to continue being as transparent with her own journey as she is, and continues to choose to be. But I was finally transparent with my whole journey because of her. I was set free. And in that freedom, I know that story is going to help inspire hope to so many more fighting to find their voice, fighting to find His.

I know that Voice is going to lead me forward. I don't know what it's going to look like, but He does! Her courage gave me courage to do what I thought was the impossible—now *that*'s a leader.

If you're looking for freedom in any area of your life, this is where you will find it. Back in Chapter 1, I told you to find me. Well, now it's up to you. Will you?

CHAPTER 25

"What's Your Story?"

The Overcomers:
I'm Not The Only One With A Story

What you've read is just one story. I know I'm not the only person with a story, and my story isn't the only one where that Voice, has been working, doing the miraculous.

I know there are countless stories all over the world. Stories that could inspire hope into the hurting inspire faith into the faithless; Stories that might reach the hearts my story won't reach. But that's the beauty of gathering all of us together. Together, we can do so much more and help so many more.

What's your story? What are the broken cracks, with

which that Voice filled with GOLD?

Did you know that, in Japan, broken ceramic dishes are often repaired with liquid gold? The flaw is seen as a unique piece of the object's history, which adds to its beauty. I love that. To me, it symbolizes what that Voice does with the brokenness in each of our lives. Like He did with me. I believe those cracks, and the "gold" He fills them with, are what creates the most powerful and inspirational stories. The Voice wants to fill every single crack in your life with something beautiful.

Think of this as the origin story of a new group of heroes I'll call *The Overcomers.* It's on my heart to help tell more stories of what that Voice (that Gold) has done to repair cracked lives. If you've loved hearing this story, we invite you to join the adventure of discovering more hope and belief that there's something out there bigger than ourselves. Who knows? it might even inspire you, as you go through your own season of brokenness, that you, too, can overcome.

I believe in your story.

I believe that God—that Voice—wants to do the same for you (I bet He has already started). If you've got a story to share, I'd love to hear it! I believe in you. And I believe that where you're currently at is not the end, but rather, just the beginning of all that He, wants to do. That Voice loves you far more than you can imagine.

Join us on social media, and the interwebs, as we now help others tell their stories.

Let's come together as ***The Overcomers.***

Let's change the world, one life at a time.

JOIN THE MOVEMENT

Do you know an Overcomer? Let us know! But more importantly, the world needs to know about them. Do you know someone who has Overcome loss, tragedy, trauma, their past, etc. Let's HONOR them. Will you help us?

Record a quick 3 minute video of yourself answering the following:

1. Your name
2. WHO you think is an Overcomer (say your friend's name)
3. WHY do you think they're an Overcomer - give us a quick description of what they've overcome, speak LIFE into the victorious person you view them as.
4. Post the SHORT clip on social media and tag us! Please tag:

   Facebook: @WeBelieveInYourStory

   Instagram: @Overcomers_filledwithgold

   Hashtags: #WeBelieveInYourStory
   #TheOvercomers
   #FilledWithGold
5. After posting the video, send us their email address so we can get in touch with them!

FOR MORE INFORMATION

We want to hear from you!

Email us at:

TheOvercomersInfo@gmail.com

To stay up to date with *The Overcomers* find us at:

www.sponge-designs.com/the-overcomers

Find us on Social Media:

Facebook: @WeBelieveInYourStory

Instagram: @Overcomers_filledwithgold

Mailing Address:

Jen Horling
10040 W. Cheyenne Ave Ste. #170-250
Las Vegas NV, 89129